# The
# Choreography
## of Presenting

# Praise for *The Choreography of Presenting*

*This book is a "must-have" for your library to remind you of the essential abilities for productive communication. Strategies, cues, and other hints provide readers with clear guidance to help them be better communicators and therefore better leaders.*

**Kathy DiRanna,**
**Director, WestEd's K–12 Alliance**

*I once had an art history teacher who made his lectures come alive with hand gestures, fluctuations in voice, and a calm authority. All of the students loved the class, learned a lot, and developed an appreciation for art history. I now know many of the things that made his lectures so educational. In* **The Choreography of Presenting***, Kendall Zoller and Claudette Landry have captured many of the abilities and skills demonstrated by this great teacher. Whether you are presenting to hundreds at a conference, dozens at a workshop, several at a faculty meeting, or a single colleague, applying the lessons of this book will improve your presentation. The abilities and skills of effective presenting are described in understandable and practical terms and activities. Regardless of your current ability, this book will help you become better.*

**Rodger W. Bybee,**
**Director Emeritus, Biological Sciences Curriculum Study**

*This amazing book artfully captures the complex craft of presenting to diverse audiences. Whether you are a novice or an experienced presenter, this book will transform your performance and lead you toward becoming a virtuoso! I highly recommend it to anyone seeking to hone their presentation skills.*

**Page Keeley, Past President, National Science Teachers Association**
**Director, Maine Mathematics Science Alliance**

# The
# Choreography
## of Presenting

### The 7 Essential Abilities
### of Effective Presenters

## Kendall Zoller
## Claudette Landry

Foreword by Robert J. Garmston

**CORWIN**
A SAGE Company

*For information:*

Corwin
A SAGE Company
2455 Teller Road
Thousand Oaks, California 91320
(800) 233-9936
Fax: (800) 417-2466
www.corwin.com

SAGE India Pvt. Ltd.
B 1/I 1 Mohan Cooperative
    Industrial Area
Mathura Road, New Delhi 110 044
India

SAGE Ltd.
1 Oliver's Yard
55 City Road
London EC1Y 1SP
United Kingdom

SAGE Asia-Pacific Pte. Ltd.
33 Pekin Street #02-01
Far East Square
Singapore 048763

Printed in the United States of America

*Library of Congress Cataloging-in-Publication Data*

Zoller, Kendall.
The choreography of presenting: the 7 essential abilities of effective presenters/Kendall Zoller and Claudette Landry.
     p. cm.
Includes bibliographical references and index.
ISBN 978-1-4129-7692-3 (pbk.)

   1.  Public speaking.  I.  Landry, Claudette.  II.  Title.

PN4129.15.Z65 2010
808.5′1—dc22                              2009043853

This book is printed on acid-free paper.

12   13   14   10   9   8   7   6   5   4   3

| | |
|---|---|
| *Acquisitions Editor:* | Dan Alpert |
| *Associate Editor:* | Megan Bedell |
| *Production Editor:* | Cassandra Margaret Seibel |
| *Copy Editor:* | Sarah J. Duffy |
| *Typesetter:* | C&M Digitals (P) Ltd. |
| *Proofreader:* | Jenifer Kooiman |
| *Indexer:* | Wendy Allex |
| *Cover Designer:* | Scott Van Atta |
| *Graphic Designer:* | Karine Hovsepian |

# Contents

# Foreword

*Robert J. Garmston*

"What's going on here?" I asked myself as I read this book.

Take a walk like Alice in Wonderland as you read this desperately valuable book. Everything you thought you knew about presenting, you probably can relearn here. I speak from experience. For over a decade I have taught presentation skills; written two books on the topic; attended workshops conducted by the guru of nonverbals, Michael Grinder; and cotrained with both of this book's authors, including doing a trial-by-fire training with Kendall with police officers, some of whom in the beginning didn't want to be in the training yet by the end were willing and happy participants. I kept asking myself, "What is going on here? I'm supposed to be writing a foreword for this book, but it is taking me ages because I keep stopping and writing notes for myself."

The authors have put together a state-of-the-art treatise on communications as it pertains to presenting to and facilitating groups. Their work is supported by research and delightful stories—we've all been there—some good and some bad experiences with groups that they use to illustrate preferred ways of gaining rapport, establishing credibility, conveying information, enhancing learning, energizing and focusing groups, and dealing with the challenging behaviors that come up periodically with an errant individual or group.

If as a presenter you are currently hot, or if you are not, you can enhance your effectiveness with groups by reading this book. And have more fun. Learn, for example, how to stop looking at details and look for patterns instead to make assessments about a group's state of mind in the moment; learn to choreograph your words with nonverbal patterns to acknowledge resistance, effectively having groups leaning forward in their seats wanting to participate; learn how to listen to questions—this is where the best of us lose credibility if we don't know some simple patterns for hearing and responding to participants' questions.

And about Alice. This book captures the wonder of the imaginative world of Alice in Wonderland—but here we read about real and verifiable phenomena. Not even the Mad Hatter would have guessed that the position in which you hold your palm makes a difference in audience reception, or that freezing a gesture holds audience attention while you pause, and that those presenters who pause longer and with greater frequency are more influential.

In short, enjoy this special book. It is one you will want to keep on your shelf and return to repeatedly, internalizing and using more and more of the wonderful nonverbal science presented here.

*August 2009*
*Robert J. Garmston, Professor Emeritus,*
*California State University, Sacramento,*
*and codeveloper of Cognitive Coaching and*
*The Adaptive Schools*

# Preface

*Learning is not attained by chance. It must be sought for with ardor and attended to with diligence.*

Abigail Adams

Learning is a social event, and effective presenters provide the social glue that binds groups together in the learning environment. Music and dance are cultural glues that bind people together. All cultures dance as a way of connecting spiritually and emotionally and to transmit culture, story, and learning from one generation to the next; dance is the language of the soul. When music starts, you feel the beat. Dance steps flash through your mind; choices are made and the dance begins. Exhilarating, exciting, intimate—dance is the ultimate expression of nonverbal communication in humans. It gives us the social permission to be physically closer to a person than we might otherwise be in a casual or business conversation. Dance allows us the flexibility to either follow our partner or lead. Led by a skillful dancer, other dancers enter into a state of flow, a mental state that positive psychologist Mihály Csíkszentmihályi (2003) defines as an operation in which a person is fully immersed in what she is doing by a feeling of energized focus, full involvement, and success in the process of the activity. This book is about creating that flow during your presentations.

Dance can include two people; it can include an entire room or even a stadium. Who among us has not experienced the energy of a live concert where thousands were engaged in dance? Now that is whole-room dancing! Rapport, group dynamics, and connectedness are through the roof in situations like these and together make for a very eventful and memorable experience.

You may be reading this book because you provide professional development to adult groups within your organization or to other organizations. You know the importance of being a subject matter expert.

You also know that subject matter expertise is not enough if you want every professional learning experience to be successful. How intrigued would you be if we told you that all effective presenters have in common specific dance steps they use to accelerate the development of rapport, positive group dynamics, and participant learning? What if while reading this book you discover that by using these skills you can dramatically increase your influence and effectiveness when teaching and presenting to adult groups? Would you be interested? Who would not say "Yes!" to that?

The choreography of presenting is about the choices we have made and can make to enhance the learning of participants when presenting to our peers, colleagues, and other adult groups. In the classic book *How to Make Meetings Work,* Doyle and Strauss (1976) describe the presenter's challenge as "a combination tap dance, shuffle, and tango to a syncopated rhythm produced by unpredictable humans" (p. 89). The presenter's skills, knowledge, and abilities are the kindling that ignites participants' passion for learning. At the core of this quote from Doyle and Strauss are fundamental beliefs we have about presenting and facilitating. One core belief is that each of us only has control over ourselves. Another is that each individual is unique in the ways he views the world and learns. With these two core beliefs, we are able to work from a conscious framework that, by being flexible, conscious, and strategic with the tools contained in this book, we can design and deliver presentations that target learning in everyone.

As we watch a well-choreographed dance, the seemingly effortless movements are fluid, graceful, and purposeful. The same can be said of an effective presentation. The session has just the right rhythm, cadence, and timing. Hours of practice, rehearsal, and skills are essential for each performance. Dance is a powerful metaphor for effective presenting because dance is about leading and following, building rapport and trust, sharing passions, and living the moment.

We are not advocating that good presenters are formulaic, yet there is a formula. After all, there are specific steps to a tango, yet not all tangos look alike. It is here, in each step, that the deeper connection lives between the dancer and the audience. It happens in real time, and you adjust in real time according to the conditions, your state of mind, your intentions, and your goals. There is freedom to choose. The better the dance is understood and executed, the greater the experience for everyone involved.

Like dancing, presenting has patterns, and you adjust to the changing patterns—sometimes leading, sometimes following. You have a plan and know the destination. The plan is the scope and sequence of the workshop. It may contain a PowerPoint presentation along with a participant packet. Once you begin, however, constant microadjustments in your live performance are essential if you want the experience to be memorable for participants. This book is about seeing and learning the patterns of communication that effective presenters use. For many, these are patterns we have always looked at yet may have never actually seen or fully understood. In the following chapters we pull the curtain back to reveal the previously invisible structure of the choreography of presenting.

The tools and strategies described in this book provide the details of a micromodel of communication that can be applied to any presentation and with any audience. By employing these skills and strategies, you will enable participants in your sessions to experience positive group dynamics and to learn more, and more quickly, because you have created an optimum learning environment. Two elements that contribute to an optimum learning environment—what Renatte and Geoffrey Caine (1994) call *relaxed alertness*—are emotional safety and cognitive challenge.

Whatever your definition of a good presenter is, this book is designed to challenge and expand it. It does not teach you tricks or tips for presenting or how to prepare a presentation. Nor does it teach you how to make a PowerPoint slide, use a laser pointer, or create attractive handouts. Rather, this book is about becoming more conscious, purposeful, intentional, and present in the moment when presenting or facilitating.

All journeys have a destination, and we believe that choice lives within the journey. The more extensive your repertoire, the more options you have and the more successful you are as a presenter. The framework of the repertoire has multiple levels: the specific skills, their contexts (when they are effective, not effective, when to be proactive and reactive), patterns, and the ability to recognize and react to them. Navigating through the unpredictable while anticipating potential challenges to seek alternative paths is best facilitated when you have a set of tools that you can consciously access. The better you know these skills and their applications, the more likely your success.

When presenting to adults, your subject matter expertise is important; however, knowing how to present and how to react to the unpredictability of participants is more important in terms of making a difference in participant learning. If it is only about content and subject matter, why meet? People can read the content on their own. So why do we meet in order to learn? Because learning is a social event, it is a conscious act whose level of achievement is directly proportional to the ardent diligence the learner brings. We believe the passion for learning is facilitated, nurtured, and developed by the dance that the skilled presenter engages in. It is the dance that creates and sustains relationship, between participants and presenter and among participants. This complex and dynamically rich social intranet of learning is the dance, and the choreography determines its level of success.

Have you ever had an event in your professional life that resulted in a personal transformation so profound that your newly discovered frame of mind resulted in a new clarity? You can think of it as discovering a new universe right in front of you that you had always looked at yet never seen. Our hunch is that each of us has at least one in our life. Here is a story about one of those events from Kendall's perspective.

## FIRST CONTACT

In January 1993, I was promoted to a science curriculum coordinator position for a large school district in California. In that role, professional development, curriculum development, assessment, and standards emerged as focal points of responsibility. In February, the director of curriculum asked me to come to her office. With excitement beaming from her eyes and a welcome rhythm to her voice, Lynda told me I would be attending a five-day session on nonverbal classroom management by a wonderful presenter. She went on about how fantastic the presenter was and that she was sending me so that I could bring the content back to the district to provide training to classroom teachers.

The idea of attending a five-day session on nonverbal classroom management was not on my list of the 100 things I want to do before I die. After all, I thought with smug arrogance, I was the science coordinator and wanted to attend workshops on inquiry, on hands-on science, and learn real stuff about how our universe works. Besides, I grew up in Los Angeles in the 1970s and was familiar with Erhard Seminars Training, transcendental meditation, encounter groups, and body language. In fact, I even told my boss about these experiences and said, "Come on, I don't think learning about body language is going to be useful; it's all a cliché anyway. Besides I grew up in L.A. and know all that." As I reflect back now I think, how smug. I also realize now how encouraging, forward thinking, and wonderful Lynda was because that event changed everything.

So I anticipated this five-day training with my customary dread and reluctance, despite reports that the presenter, Michael Grinder, was very good and that his work was sound. On a cool spring morning in March, I arrived at the training site and wondered how I would endure five days of this stuff. The session was to start at 8:30. As the start time grew near, sitting in the back row near the door, I grew more angry and frustrated, thinking, "This is five days I won't get back!"

Little did I know that a transformation in the way I thought about presenting, delivering presentations, teaching, and learning had begun. About 15 minutes before the session formally began, the presenter greeted each of us and moved about the room with deliberate moves. He moved like a dancer, effortlessly shifting his steps and becoming a colleague and peer when he came to greet us, instantly developing rapport with each of us. I say rapport, but at that time in my life I did not have a name for it or a way of describing it. By the end of the first hour, I knew something significant was happening. My reluctance shifted to keenness, and my resistance shifted to an embrace of the content that started the wonderful lifelong journey that continues to this day.

What made such a difference? It was not just the content. Yes, the content was solid and good quality, but initially I did not want it. Had I heard all those messages before? Of course! But it was the presenter's dance that made the most significant difference in my receptivity and openness to consider what he had to offer. And it was not that the presenter sang and danced. As Bennis and Biederman (1988) say in *Organizing Genius,* "one can sing and dance. Or one can create an environment in which singers and dancers flourish" (p. 70). In this workshop, I watched the presenter's song and dance, consciously unaware that he was also creating an environment in which we participants flourished and learned to sing and dance to the tune of classroom management.

As I sat in this workshop, I realized that my own internal resistance and skepticism ebbed, as did that of others in the room. Most important, I realized that the shift in my thinking, my attitude, and my participation was in response to the presenter's nonverbal moves. At the end of the first day, I had a glimpse of a great presenter leading a great workshop and I was beginning to see things in ways I never had before. I began to see the interplay of communication patterns between presenter and audience and the presenter's skillful ability to choreograph his steps to support our learning every step of the way.

The presenter created a learning environment in which we flourished because we felt as if we were his partners—being a partner is essential to constructing meaning. As he changed his steps, we changed with him. As we changed our steps, he changed with us. Ever respectful and entertaining, he kept a keen eye focused on our learning. That gifted presenter demonstrated what Doyle and Strauss (1976) recognize as a challenge, the ability to do "a combination tap dance, shuffle, and tango to a syncopated rhythm produced by unpredictable humans" (p. 89). What the presenter did can be reduced to a single idea: he was respectful to the audience. The skill sets he mastered and demonstrated were the steps that make up the dance of the presenter. What does honoring an audience look, sound, and feel like? This book will lead you through the steps of this exquisite dance.

❖

## ABOUT THIS BOOK

In the chapters ahead, we explicitly describe how to plan, think, choreograph, and dance like a presenter. We are not talking about presenters who want to just get through the presentation and look good while doing it. Nor are we talking about presenters who merely talk to showcase their expertise. Effective presenting, like dancing, doesn't just appear in our midst. It has to be planned and adjusted in the moment—a challenge that runs counter to the powerful urge for some to simply rely on their content expertise or on the coattails of their own charisma. Given that presenters are experts in their field does not necessarily make them experts at presenting. Leo Tolstoy famously contended that "All happy families resemble one another; every unhappy family is unhappy in its own way." We contend that effective presenters are all alike, and all ineffective presenters are ineffective in their own way.

This book unpacks and describes the skills that effective presenters have in common. When used effectively, these skills can increase the good and decrease, if not eliminate, the negative impact of unpredictable situations and disruptive behaviors found in all settings where people come together to learn and to conduct business. By learning and practicing these skills, you will become more conscious of the profound influence these patterns have on participant learning, rapport, and relationship. When used congruently and appropriately, these skills can significantly enhance the delivery of presentations.

This book describes how to think like a presenter—leading to proficiency in declarative, procedural, and conditional knowledge. Effective presenters know what to do, how to do it, and, most important, when and if to do it. The what, when, and how of nonverbal and verbal patterns are dependent on specific content and contextual knowledge as well as a high level of proficiency at understanding and influencing group dynamics.

Our focus on the similarities among all effective presenters is framed in the 7 Essential Abilities of Effective Presenters, which incorporate both verbal and nonverbal patterns of communication and can be learned and mastered in order to effectively address the wide range of behaviors that participants display.

Humans are unpredictable, therefore it is unlikely that a presenter can consistently predict what participants are going to say or how they are going to respond or react to a given situation. What is predictable, however, like a changing dance step, is that there is a menu of plausible participant behaviors that can positively or negatively influence a presentation. Some negative behaviors may include asking many questions, side-talking with a neighbor, processing out loud, sending text messages, reading e-mail, or playing Sudoku. The gifted presenter, adept in the skills described in this book, has a vast repertoire of strategies that effectively engage participants, increasing the likelihood of participation and interaction while allowing flexibility during those unpredictable moments.

To enhance your learning while reading this book, we embrace a model from the arts. Artists practice, and practice usually entails a focus on individual skills and moves. Next, they rehearse. Rehearsal is a safe learning environment in which performers put their skills to test in real-life simulations. After many practices and rehearsals comes the performance. The performance is your presentation. We submit that the work you do in this book, in the practice sessions and rehearsals, will make a difference in the quality of your presentations and in the learning of those who attend. Engaging in deliberate and focused practice and rehearsals contributes to a well-executed performance. By learning and practicing these skills, you will become more conscious of the profound influence that these communication patterns have on participant learning, rapport, and receptivity. When used congruently and appropriately, these skills will significantly enhance the delivery of your next presentation by elevating your craftsmanship and providing you with a toolbox for navigating the unexpected.

# Acknowledgments

Corwin gratefully acknowledges the contributions of the following reviewers:

Art Costa, Professor Emeritus
California State University, Sacramento, CA

Beverly Ginther, Staff Development Coordinator
Minnetonka Public Schools, Minnetonka, MN

Lloyd Kajikawa, Administrator
Los Angeles County Office of Education, Downey, CA

Cindy C. Kratzer, Literacy Coordinator
SMMUSD Educational Services, Santa Monica, CA

Pam Hankins, Codirector of Staff Development
Springfield Public Schools, Springfield, MO

Rob Kesselring, Speaker and Workshop Leader
Uncommon Seminars, Apple Valley, MN

Terry Morganti-Fisher, Educational Consultant
Morganti Fisher Associates, Austin, TX

Primus Moore, Assistant Principal/Director
McAlester Public Schools, McAlester, OK

Susan Mundry, Deputy Director of Learning Innovations
WestEd, Woburn, MA

Julie Prescott, Assessment Coordinator
Vallivue High School, Caldwell, ID

# About the Authors

**Kendall Zoller, EdD,** is president of Sierra Training Associates and provides professional learning seminars and keynotes on facilitation and presentation skills and leadership to schools, districts, universities, state agencies, and corporations throughout North America. His international research focuses on identifying nonverbal patterns in the learning environment and their influences on thinking, memory, and learning. In 2007 he introduced Nonverbal Communicative Intelligence as a framework to explain the cognitive, neurological, physiological, behavioral, and social foundations of nonverbal communication.

He has extensive experience presenting to and coaching a diverse range of audiences, including sales teams, senior managers, university faculty and staff, law enforcement leaders, administrators, and teachers. He is a contributing author to Robert Garmston's *Presenter's Field Guide* and is a Cohort I Fellow and mentor to the National Academy for Science and Mathematics Education Leadership. Kendall may be contacted at kvzoller@ftcnet.net.

**Claudette Landry, MEd,** is the principal of an elementary school in Davis, California. She has taught all grades, from kindergarten to eighth grade, and has worked extensively with teachers in implementing effective instructional strategies and in developing collaborative communities that maximize learning and human development. She has been a leader in professional and organizational development for the past 20 years, offering workshops, trainings, and presentations at the school, district, and national levels. Claudette has facilitated dialogues and discussions with groups from many different industries and fields to generate common understandings and to develop go-ahead strategies for overcoming challenges. She keeps teams task focused and goal oriented by further developing group members' communication, presentation, and facilitation skills.

# Introduction to the 7 Essential Abilities of Effective Presenters

*The newest computer can merely compound, at speed, the oldest problem in the relations between human beings, and in the end the communicator will be confronted with the old problem, of what to say and how to say it.*

Edward R. Murrow

All effective presenters establish credibility; build and sustain rapport; read the group; balance task, process, and group development; listen to and acknowledge participants; respond appropriately; and recover with grace. Combined, these abilities make up the cornerstone necessary to dance masterfully. Within each of these 7 abilities are five to eight specific skills and moves. Consequently, we describe more than 50 discrete skills in the chapters that follow. This book is organized around the 7 Essential Abilities, each of which corresponds to a particular chapter.

### Essential Ability 1: Establish Credibility
This lays the foundation for participants to attribute intelligence, competence, confidence, and expertise to the presenter. Credibility is a presenter characteristic perceived and assigned by the group. The specific

---

**7 Essential Abilities of Effective Presenters**

- Establish credibility
- Build and sustain rapport
- Read the group
- Balance task, process, and group development
- Listen to and acknowledge participants
- Respond appropriately
- Recover with grace

---

skills associated with credibility include voice tone, use of the still gesture, credible stance, and abdominal breathing patterns.[1]

### Essential Ability 2: Build and Sustain Rapport

This involves strategies and moves that create a short-term psychological state in which the lines of communication are wide open. When rapport is high, participants are cognitively responsive and therefore receptive to considering new understandings that challenge their current models of knowing. Knowing how to establish rapport, break rapport, and reestablish rapport are critical skills in the learning environment that support student thinking and problem solving.[2]

### Essential Ability 3: Read the Group

This entails recognizing, processing, and responding to participants' nonverbal patterns. The presenter reads the group to anticipate their learning needs as well as their psychological and physiological needs. By reading the nonverbal behaviors of participants, an effective presenter can anticipate resistance, recognize receptivity, and choreograph facilitation moves that support positive group dynamics.

### Essential Ability 4: Balance Task, Process, and Group Development

This involves an interaction between outcomes (task), protocols (process), and relationship (group development). Effectively balancing the three ensures acquiring a tangible outcome while promoting maximum learning and optimal participation in the time available.

### Essential Ability 5: Listen to and Acknowledge Participants

This involves deliberate steps in a delicate dance. Adults offer several challenges in learning environments, one of which is the willingness to reveal what they know and don't know as well as what they are learning. Effective listening requires Ability 2 (Build and Sustain Rapport) as well as specific voice, eye, gesture, and stance patterns to give participants the perception of being sincerely listened to and acknowledged. Participant engagement and learning depends on being understood and having the sense of feeling safe enough to divulge their thinking to the group.

### Essential Ability 6: Respond Appropriately

This is dependent on the effective implementation of the skills related to Ability 5. When a person feels listened to and acknowledged, the effective presenter can then deliver an appropriate response. Responding appropriately requires evaluating, synthesizing, and delivering a congruent verbal and nonverbal message. It is about making the person and the group *right*, by which we mean feeling safe to be wrong, to reveal learning, and to reveal what they do not know.

### Essential Ability 7: Recover With Grace

This involves the ability to recognize when the participants stop thinking and you have lost group rapport or group attention, or perhaps even just lost your place. Graceful nonverbal moves ensure that the group will stay present, focused, and engaged. This intriguing ability includes the nonverbal moves associated with changing location, pausing, gestures of location, and stance.

---

**Reflection 1** | **Exploring the 7 Essential Abilities**

To more effectively engage in the 7 Essential Abilities, take some time to complete the following reflection.

**Step 1:** Begin by reading the first ability again. Then, to surface your interpretation, paraphrase it in your own words.

**Step 2:** Think of a situation you observed in which you noticed an effective presenter using that ability.

**Step 3:** Repeat Steps 1 and 2 for each of the 7 Essential Abilities.

---

The patterns within the 7 Essential Abilities are ubiquitous in communication; people use them constantly and seamlessly at an unconscious or habitual level. By reading this book, you may experience a new consciousness in your own patterns—patterns that up until now you have always engaged in but perhaps never recognized. The gift of consciousness is not only found in recognizing the patterns, but also in developing your perceptual acuity to recognize the influence these patterns have on your communication and how improved your relationships will become. Patterns of nonverbal communication are used by everyone and unconsciously understood by most. The enculturation of nonverbal patterns in communication is tacit in nature, and only a few written texts of rules and descriptors exist. Michael Grinder, a colleague, mentor, and friend, has authored several useful nonacademic books defining these patterns, including *ENVoY: Your Personal Guide to Classroom Management* (1993) for teachers and *The Elusive Obvious* (2008). Readers familiar with Grinder will recognize the parallel and interweaving ideas between his work and the 7 Essential Abilities. For the academically inclined, the most complete academic text on nonverbal patterns of communication within and across cultures is the three-volume magnum opus *Nonverbal Communication Across Disciplines*, by the linguist Fernando Poyatos (2002a, 2002b, 2002c).

You may discover some intriguing connections between the information in this book and things you already know. One is how intertwined the 7 Essential Abilities are with Howard Gardner's (1985) model of interpersonal intelligence. This connection is made even stronger in the model of nonverbal communicative intelligence (Zoller, 2008), in which critical thinking, problem solving, physiology, neurology, and metabolism are all interconnected and interdependent in communication. Another significant connection is found in Daniel Goleman's (2006) *Social Intelligence*. For Goleman, social intelligence is rooted in empathy and rapport, both of which are expressly dependent on nonverbal cues.

As you read this book, we hope that many discoveries emerge for you through the practices and rehearsals on your way to using your new learning in future presentations. It is our hunch that the value in learning will come from knowing what the skills are, why they are important, how to do them, and their potential benefits. So let's begin our own dance.

# 1

# Establish Credibility

*To be persuasive we must be believable; to be believable we must be credible; to be credible we must be truthful.*

Edward R. Murrow

Credibility is a presenter characteristic perceived and assigned by the group. The group assigns the following attributes to the credible presenter: intelligence, competence, believability, and expertise. If the presenter's intention is to be perceived as an expert who is intelligent, competent, and believable, then the choreography of nonverbal moves can be orchestrated to increase the likelihood of gaining that credibility.

This is not to suggest that credibility will be established by simply implementing specific nonverbal patterns without having any actual expertise in a discipline. Nor will it be established if the presenter knows the content intimately and naïvely believes all that is necessary to impress an audience and gain credibility is expertise in a field or discipline. The presenter must be an expert both in the field and in presenting. The first few minutes of any presentation are crucial to actuate credibility as well as to increase the probability that a group will be receptive to the message. Actuating credibility is supported by the deliberate, strategic, and effective use of nonverbal skills.

Many books about presentation skills recommend establishing credibility early in a presentation. What does it look like and sound like when a presenter is credible? What specific actions increase the probability that a group will assign credibility to the presenter? How long does it take to build credibility, and how do you know when you've achieved it in the eyes of the audience?

1

Let's think first about some people that many of us perceive as credible—in other words, we consider them intelligent, competent, and believable, and what they say is what they mean to say. This does not imply that we all agree with their views; remember that nonverbal moves can establish credibility even when others disagree with your idea. The following are interesting examples of people who demonstrate use of credible voice tone: the late newscaster Peter Jennings, former British Prime Minister Tony Blair, and former U.S. Secretary of State Madeleine Albright. Remember, we are not necessarily saying that they are credible; rather, they consistently model a credible voice tone and the visual indicators of credibility. In the acting arena, Meryl Streep, Jane Alexander, George C. Scott, James Earl Jones, and Denzel Washington often portray highly credible characters. A good friend considers Clint Eastwood's Inspector Harry Callahan as the most credible character he knows—"Go ahead, make my day."

Each of these people is highly skilled at choosing the appropriate voice, stance, pause, gesture, and breathing. Each of these nonverbal moves, when used proficiently, increases credibility. By being conscious of these five skills, a presenter can succeed at establishing credibility despite perhaps not being initially viewed as credible.

## THE FIRST IMPRESSION

A teacher who attended our training on essential abilities for presenters sent us an e-mail describing her success at establishing credibility. Natasha worked in a large urban school district, and with three years of classroom experience she accepted a curriculum coordinator position. She was nervous prior to her first meeting with the high school department chairs because she knew she had this one chance to set the stage for credibility and lay the groundwork for trust in front of more experienced and senior colleagues. She consciously prepared her opening for the meeting by scripting her verbal and nonverbal message with the intent of gaining credibility from the group.

As Natasha began the meeting, she took a deep, relaxing breath and stood still with her weight evenly distributed and her feet about hip distance apart. Her arms were at her side, her hands relaxed. As she began to speak, she made eye contact with those in the room and spoke in a voice that was relatively narrow in pitch. With each important point, the tone of her voice subtly dropped in a synchronized cadence on the last word of each phrase. In the first 90 seconds, the stage was set for a successful meeting. Natasha had a successful meeting, and she attributed her success to the deliberate and conscious use of voice, gesture, stance, pause, and breathing.

Knowing the five skills linked to credibility is not enough; you also need to recognize what each skill looks and sounds like as well as when to use it. In the remainder of this chapter, each of these skills is isolated and described in distinct detail. Although we will "teach'" each skill in isolation, in reality no skill stands alone. So keep in mind that nonverbal signals and the words you speak evolve from the choreography of individual skills combined in a complementary dance. Effective presentations depend on a careful blending of these skills.

## VOICE

Each of us has a range in voice pitch that can be used effectively depending on the intended outcome. Voice pitch can be consciously selected based on deliberate intention. By changing your voice tone, you can change the meaning of the word and influence the listeners' perceptions. In languages around the world, the linguist Fernanado Poyatos (2002a) found that changes in pitch determine the meaning of a word. Adam Kendon (2004), another linguist, linked voice tone and gesture to perceptions of authority and compassion. As with Grinder's (1993) model, we can think of voice range as existing on a continuum from approachable to credible (Figure 1.1). One end is associated with a rhythmic intonation that is often associated with the intent to seek information. This is called *approachable voice*. Presenters use this voice pattern when seeking information, posing questions, or asking participants to consider an idea. Using the approachable voice, presenters build positive relationships that encourage participation by creating a psychologically safe environment with strong rapport.

Figure 1.1    Voice Pitch Continuum

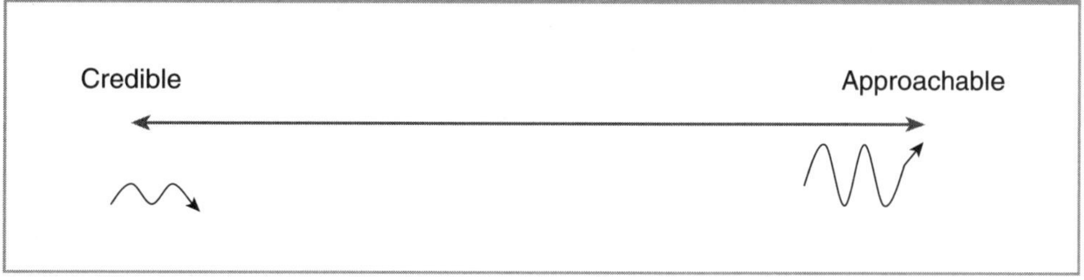

Credible

Approachable

On the other end of the continuum is a voice characterized by a more narrow modulation in pitch, which is often associated with sending information or giving directions. This is called *credible voice*. Presenters often use this voice when they want to be definitive, give instructions for an activity, and establish credibility. By using the credible voice, presenters can more effectively amplify important content, give directions, and inform. Each voice along the continuum is used purposefully and with intent. By developing conscious awareness of your initial voice range and a willingness to expand that range, you can have greater influence on participants during seminars, workshops, trainings, classes, and keynotes.[3]

Table 1.1 illustrates the visual indicators of approachable and credible voice patterns. The auditory indicators of an approachable voice pattern are characterized by rhythmic tonal variation and a rise in pitch at the end of the sentence. Smooth, fluent, and rhythmic, these kinesic and aural features increase the likelihood that the presenter will be perceived as invitational. The quality of participants' interpretations and understandings is enhanced through the congruent use of the presenter's verbal and nonverbal patterns.

The auditory indicators of a credible voice pattern include a flattening of pitch, with little deviation from a baseline, and often a drop in pitch at the end of a sentence or phrase. These patterns are on a continuum, so the more credible the voice, the less the head moves and the flatter the rhythm of the voice. The extreme end of this continuum is represented by complete stillness while talking until the final chin drop at the end of each phrase. As long as there is calm breathing accompanied with credible voice, there is strong likelihood that the presenter will be perceived as credible. Retired newscaster Tom Brokaw was a master of this pattern.

**Table 1.1**  Visual Indicators of Voice Patterns

| Approachable | Credible |
|---|---|
| Head bobs | Head is relatively still |
| Chin often rises at the end of a phrase or sentence | Chin often drops at the end of a phrase or sentence |
| Gestures are fluid, palms often facing up | Gestures tend to be more still, palms often parallel to the ground or facing down |
| Gestures are slow relative to personal baseline | Gestures are fast relative to personal baseline |
| Speaker tends to blink more | Speaker tends to blink less |
| Speaker often leans forward | Speaker often maintains erect posture |
| Weight may be on one leg more than other | Weight is often distributed evenly on both feet |

### Practice 1.1 | Approachable Voice

Say the following sentence while bobbing your head to add rhythm to the pitch in your voice.
*As you consider what you have just read, what do you think might come next?*

### Practice 1.2 | Credible Voice

Say the following sentence while holding your head fairly still and narrowing the pitch of your voice. Be sure to drop the pitch at the end phrase.
*As you take out your books, turn to page 42.*

Two factors are important when thinking about becoming a more effective presenter. First is recognizing that each skill can be represented on a continuum. Knowing the range of the continuum is useful because it allows freedom in the implementation of each skill. The second important point is being aware of your range along the continuum for each skill. By recognizing your habitual range, you can deliberately increase the usefulness of a skill to be of greater influence on your audience. Increasing the range of verbal and nonverbal skills offers greater potential to be of influence with the rich diversity of participants attending your sessions.

Now that you have experienced the two extreme voice ranges, the next step is to explore when to use each one. Context determines which to use. When the intention is to seek information from participants or to have another person participate, it is most effective to use the approachable voice. When sending information, providing instructions, or managing behavior, it makes more sense to use the credible voice. In Practice 1.3, you will say the same message twice, first with an approachable voice and then with a credible voice. By doing this, you will experience both congruence and incongruence. Incongruence results from the mismatch between what is said and the nonverbal pattern used. Congruence is achieved when the verbal message and nonverbal pattern are matched, or rather, aligned.

### Practice 1.3 | Matching Intention With Voice

Congruence: say the following statement in an approachable voice.
*You're suggesting the westward movement was in part developed through manifest destiny?*
Incongruence: say the following statement in a credible voice.

*(Continued)*

(Continued)

*You're suggesting the westward movement was in part developed through manifest destiny?*

Reflection: in the space below, write your thoughts about the influence of these voice patterns on the perceived meaning of these sentences.

## STANCE

For adults there are few things simpler than standing. Interestingly, it is one of the most difficult moves to describe in writing. We realize that the majority of our readers have been standing, with varying degrees of success, since about the age of one. What you may not realize, however, is that your stance may very well influence your audience's perception of your credibility. It may surprise you how difficult it is to learn a new stance. When asked to change your stance, it feels not only contrived, but also artificial and uncomfortable. Claudette struggled for several months to develop a more credible stance when presenting that differed from her default stance. By using her newly acquired credible stance, she found that she was better able to quickly win participants' attention, maintain their interest, and keep them focused on the content for longer periods of time using less effort than she did before perfecting this skill.

### 5 Elements of the Credible Stance

1. Feet are parallel and hip-distance apart.

2. Arms may be perpendicular to the ground, or the lower arm may be held such that it is parallel to the ground. Both arms held such that the lower arms are parallel to the ground also constitutes a credible stance.

3. Breathe abdominally, calmly, deeply.

4. Stand still, no rocking back and forth.

5. Maintain an erect yet relaxed posture.

There are five elements to consider when implementing a credible stance: placement of your feet, placement of your arms, your breathing, stillness, and your posture. To have a credible stance, place your feet hip-distance apart, with weight evenly distributed on both feet. Stand still, with your back straight, arms relaxed at your side and with your hands open and fingers slightly curved and relaxed. As you breathe calmly and deeply from the abdomen, your shoulders will automatically drop even before you open your mouth. The calm, deep breathing and relaxed shoulders contribute to an internal state of relaxed alertness. The group will perceive you to be a confident and competent speaker.

When you use the credible voice coupled with the proper stance when delivering content, the audience begins to attribute these qualities to content expertise and they will tend to ask fewer questions while you are delivering content, thus reducing interruption to the flow. This pattern reduces the number of interruptions because it is linked to participants' auditory processing. The audience will be more attentive, less distracted, and more likely to receive clear and resonant communications. As they listen and absorb content, questions emerging from inattention or daydreaming will almost cease.

---

## LOSING MY WAY

We observed a teacher presenting to the staff at a large urban high school. The teacher, Louie, standing with one hand in his pocket and the other resting on the podium, introduced the first major topic of the morning. He leaned forward as he spoke and used a monotone voice with little inflection. To our surprise, the stance he used in front of his peers was nothing like the credible and commanding stance he used in front of his students when teaching. In the classroom he was effective, was well liked, and had great rapport with his students. During the first five minutes of his presentation to peers, however, several hands went up and he began taking questions. After responding to a few, he murmured under his breath, "Let's see, where am I?" It took him a few minutes to get back on track; in that time the group's attention decreased and his credibility was lost. As a result of being distracted by their questions, Louie wasted time because he had to repeat information and did not have the participants' unstated permission to hold their questions until a more appropriate time. The group momentum, or energy, and rapport became disrupted. The flow of information got interrupted, and Louie got flustered and lost his train of thought regarding the next important point he was going to make. Ultimately he did recover, but he used up valuable time.

In your workplace, time is among the most limited of resources. Very few professionals have more time available than work to be done. Implementing an effective stance is a first step to gaining credibility, and establishing credibility ultimately saves time when it comes to delivering information or teaching content.

In contrast to Louie, we saw another, this time skillful, presenter speak to university faculty about effective teaching strategies in the college classroom. When Alicia delivered content about teaching, she stood still, with weight evenly distributed on both feet. Her range of voice modulation was narrow, and her pitch dropped with each important point. The audience was attentive and engaged during the 15-minute segment. She moved slowly and silently from where she delivered the content to a different location a few feet away. From this new location, Alicia called for questions and responded to each in a way that created comfort and understanding in the group. Then, with a pause and slow walking speed, she returned to her original delivery location and began the next topic. Alicia expertly established two locations, one for content and another for questions. As you will discover in Chapters 4 and 5, location is an important quality to consider when listening to and acknowledging participants. Location is also valuable when recovering with grace.

These two stories offer a contrast that illustrates the influence that the individual components of credibility have on group behavior. The effective implementation of the 7 Essential Abilities in Alicia's story illustrates several positive outcomes: the participants assigned credibility to the presenter, the presentation moved with a synergistic flow, and the presentation supported participants' thinking and met intended outcomes within the allotted meeting time.

## PAUSE

*The right word may be effective, but no word was ever as effective as a rightly timed pause.*

Mark Twain

The pause is yet another nonverbal skill used effectively by Alicia. When presenting, the pause is not an empty silence, rather, as Poyatos (2002b) describes, it is an interactive segment between the presenter and audience that is filled with meaning and influence. According to Grinder (1997), the pause is the single most effective nonverbal pattern. What makes it so effective is that, more than any other single nonverbal skill, it has the greatest influence on the metabolism of the listener. In fact, when talking with another person, if the speaker pauses and stops breathing for a longer-than-normal breath, the other person will also stop breathing. We are not advocating that you hold your breath to get someone else to stop breathing. This example simply shows how connected we are to one another when conversing.

The pause, unique in its diverse applications, has many purposes. Consider using it in the following situations when presenting:

1. Before making an important point to gain the group's attention

2. After making an important point to support thinking by members in the audience

3. In the middle of a sentence to get the group's attention (a management application)

4. To stop side talking while you are presenting

5. Before asking an important question to generate anticipation

6. After someone responds to give you time to think

The pause can be used to establish credibility because it can increase the group's perception of a presenter's intelligence, thoughtfulness, passion, and empathy. It supports thinking and is an effective technique to indirectly get attention and manage groups.

The pause is most effective when it is accompanied by a still stance, calm breathing, indirect eye contact, and a frozen hand gesture. The combination of these four elements is so influential because the brain is hardwired to pay attention to pattern shifts. Recognizing pattern shifts is an essential part of our survival mechanism. Long ago, early humans might have gazed attentively across the swaying grasses of the savannah. Noticing a specific movement different from the swaying grasses (a pattern shift) would cause focus and attention on that change—it could be a lion stalking or prey fleeing. The ability to detect and discern differences and shifts in patterns has remained constant among humans to the present day. When presenting, those in the audience may not be lions or prey, but human neurology recognizes and responds in the training room as it did on the savannah. Skilled presenters understand how to use specific nonverbal patterns to gain attention without verbally asking for it by creating pattern shifts.

The pause can be used deliberately to circuitously manage adult groups, and this is an important skill to perfect as a presenter. Most adults take offense at being directly managed. When they perceive direct management during a presentation, their emotional resourcefulness decreases, substantially reducing the presenter's effectiveness. The successful managing of adults is best served through indirect nonverbal techniques as opposed to direct verbal commands. Consider when side talk occurs during a presentation. An ineffective presenter may stop talking and look directly at the guilty party. As the group's attention shifts from the presenter to the focus of the presenter's ire, they become more and more uncomfortable by the overt management of the presenter. This power move by the presenter lessens his or her credibility and often causes participants to shift uncomfortably in their seats, decreasing the group's receptivity and rapport.

The more skilled presenter, when noticing side talk, would confront side talk in a different way. As the presenter speaks, he strategically and intentionally interrupts himself during a multisyllabic word, which causes a larger pattern shift than merely stopping between words. In addition to the interruption, a pause follows the incomplete word. The presenter might shift to indirect eye contact as opposed to direct eye contact to lessen the degree of direct management of the group and the offenders. Implementing this skill set often results in the immediate cessation of side talk. Because the presenter is not looking at the guilty party, neither the group nor the talkers perceive that they are being managed. The side talk simply stops, and everyone starts paying attention again. In short, it is indirect management that preserves relationship and rapport, maintains credibility, and puts the group's learning needs above individual needs.

---

### Practice 1.4 | I Interrupt Myself: A Management Skill

1. Begin a sentence, and interrupt yourself about three words into the sentence. Be sure to interrupt a multisyllabic word.

2. Pause, drop eye contact from the group, and stand still.

3. Silently take a step aside (decontaminate).

4. Snap to, and begin the sentence from the beginning with a new voice pattern (amnesia): "One very impor . . . one very important point to consider is. . . ."

---

Before the pause, the speaker is talking, breathing, looking at the group, gesturing along with the words, and perhaps even moving. When the talking, looking, gesturing, and moving stop—yet calm breathing continues—the pause will gain the group's attention. As the presenter continues to breathe calmly, so does the group, ensuring uninterrupted rapport. Physiologically, it is crucial to maintain good blood flow to the neocortex to support focus, thinking, and engagement.

## GESTURE

*Words represent your intellect. The sound, gesture, and movement represent your feelings.*

Patricia Fripp

When listening to a presenter, attention is paid to the words as well as how they are spoken. Listeners also are unconsciously drawn to the speaker's face and gestures. Humans derive meaning from the message based not only on speech, but also on facial expressions and gestures (Ekman & Friesen, 1969). The group is more likely to perceive credibility when the presenter holds gestures still while pausing. This is effective because the stillness created by the freezing of the gesture, coupled with the pause, captures the audience's attention, which in turn contributes to the group's perception of the presenter's intelligence.

The frozen or still gesture is completely congruent with the pause. A frozen hand gesture is the visual correlation to an auditory pause. Once the presenter pauses and holds a frozen gesture, there is no misinterpreting the intention of the message. To appear credible, we suggest striving for congruence between voice and gesture.

> The frozen hand gesture is the visual correlation to an auditory pause.

As noted at the outset of this section, the most effective gestures to gain credibility are those that are held still when the presenter pauses. The key to implementing an effective gesture is to coordinate it with the silent pause. This takes practice; however, once mastered, the influence and regularity of its effective use is a powerful tool when speaking. For example, U.S. President Barack Obama often effectively implements a frozen gesture during his pause. On the other hand, former U.S. President George W. Bush often paused with his mouth slightly open and his gesture held frozen through the pause and into the next sentence. Effective pausing and a frozen gesture are usually seen as credible. Yet doing so with the lips apart is often perceived as less credible. It is true now as always that what you are doing speaks so loudly that others may not hear what you say.

## BREATHING

As you develop your understanding of the importance of breathing (your own and that of your audience), it is important to explore an emerging area of brain research. Fifteen years ago in a primate lab in Italy, something extraordinary happened (Rizzolatti & Gallese, 2002). Researchers discovered that specific premotor neurons in a monkey's brain fired when the monkey saw the lab technician grab and eat a raisin. It turns out the neurons that fired in the monkey's brain fired exactly the same as they would have had the monkey actually picked up the raisin and eaten it. In a sense, the brain was mirroring neurologically what the eyes were seeing. It was actually going through the premotor process of picking up a raisin and eating it as an internal process, even though the only external action was viewing the stimuli. This marked the discovery of *mirror neurons.* A decade later, the revelation from this serendipitous event resulted in an important discovery about the human brain. In 2002, researchers from the University of Parma and the University of California, Los Angeles, discovered mirror neurons in humans; with that discovery, an onslaught of clinical applications and knowledge emerged (Stamenov & Gallese, 2002).

One significant understanding to emerge from all of this is the connection between mirror neurons and breathing. How a person breathes influences blood flow and oxygen intake, thus impacting the capacity for thinking. The presence of mirror neurons also suggests a relationship between a presenter's breathing pattern and the group's breathing pattern. If a presenter is breathing high and fast, the audience will match that pattern, releasing chemicals associated with the fight-or-flight response. The blood flow to the neocortex is reduced, and thinking becomes more difficult for the presenter as well as for the group.

Conversely, when the presenter breathes slowly, primarily using the abdominal muscles, the group will mirror that breathing pattern. By breathing this way, our neurological baseline remains intact and chemicals supporting the fight-or-flight response are not released. Sufficient oxygen and blood flow reach the neocortex, and our capacity for thinking remains functional. Additionally, a presenter exhibiting a calm breathing pattern is perceived by the audience as more confident and competent, thus creating an opportunity to establish and maintain credibility. In Chapter 2, we discuss the role of mirror neurons in the area of rapport. But first a story on breathing . . .

A colleague of ours was asked to give a one-hour presentation. Unfortunately, the host asked him to cover too much content in the allotted time. Consequently, he talked too fast, paused too little, and breathed too quickly and highly. His high breathing contributed to the audience's state of mind being less receptive than it could have been. The audience did not perceive the presenter to be credible. In fact, they perceived him as nervous and unsure of his content, as evidenced in the postseminar evaluations. In reality, the presenter had 15 years of research and presentation experience and knew his content intimately. This incongruence and the audience's perceptions were the direct result of the presenter's high breathing, rapid delivery, and insufficient pauses. Had he been congruent, the participants might have learned and retained much more from that one-hour session. Sometimes it is more effective to go slow in order to support learning.

It is essential for presenters to recognize their own breathing as well as the group's breathing. This ability allows presenters to be of greater influence with the group and is essential in establishing and maintaining credibility. A group's breathing pattern is recognizable. For example, observe a person sitting in a chair inhaling: notice that the shoulders rise a little and the head moves back ever so slightly. As she exhales, her head often moves forward and the shoulders drop slightly. The movement is subtle, yet it is perceptible at a surprising distance once you know what to look for. As suggested by Grinder (1997), another effective way to recognize inhaling and exhaling is to observe what he calls secondary evidence. For instance, when a person breathes in, he becomes larger and the clothes tend to become smoother, less wrinkled. As he exhales, the clothes wrinkle. It is also easier to enhance perceptual acuity by observing someone breathing from a side profile. From the side, you can see the head move backward and forward. Once recognized, this pattern becomes more recognizable when looking at someone straight on. The ability to perceive group breathing is learned through ongoing observation. Once learned, an important step is to know what to do when you notice either yourself or the group not breathing or breathing shallowly. This is addressed in Chapter 7.

In early 2009, just prior to the inauguration of President Barack Obama, Caroline Kennedy emerged as a candidate to fill the U.S. Senate seat vacated by Hillary Clinton. In a telling moment of monumental consequence, this Harvard-educated lawyer fell prey to public perception. It was reported by the *New York Times* that in one segment of just less than three minutes, Kennedy said "you know" no fewer than 30 times. As the interview continued, the "you knows" rapidly followed. The press and blogs had a field day calling into question her intelligence. Interestingly, had she simply paused in silence, closed her mouth, and breathed calmly, the "you know" utterances would have diminished, if not completely disappeared, and she would have been perceived as more intelligent. This skill, as simple as it seems, takes much practice.

Sometimes when presenting, you may pause to think of what to say next or to choose what word will most effectively communicate the intended content. During these cognitive pauses when you are stuck searching for a word or idea, you may become still and inadvertently stop your own breathing. It is at this time that you may utter the infamous placeholder "um" or "you know." This may be a natural verbal response to your internal deliberation and thinking; on one level, freezing your moves reduces the need for the brain to process movements, sounds, gestures, and so on. When breathing is paused, however, oxygen is no longer added to the blood. As the oxygen levels in the blood decrease, the fight-or-flight response is initiated by the release of cortisol. Blood flow is shunted away from the brain and directed to the muscles. This entire neurological and physiological process occurs in less than 20 milliseconds. The decrease of blood flow to the brain results in a decrease in the capacity to think clearly. The brain, an organ that makes up about 2% of your body mass yet consumes up to 35% of the oxygen, is a high-octane engine. When oxygen is limited, the brain functions much less efficiently.

If you pause, and then hold your breath, your thinking will dry up and the audience may become puzzled. When puzzled, participants breathe more shallowly and soon start down the same path of confusion and distraction. Even momentary lapses that impact the flow of oxygen to your brain may create the need for a retooling and a recovery skill in the training room. Unfortunately, once the brain stops thinking, those without conscious access to these skills might just "stand there." Auditory processors have been heard to say, "Now what was I going to say" or "I just lost my train of thought." Absent calling for a break, there is little else to do. The converse is to be conscious of your breathing and how it impacts that of others. Used well, it can be a cornerstone to the manner in which your audience perceives your competence and confidence—and how they assign credibility to you and what you want to say.

By pausing and not breathing, you can also inadvertently cause the audience to hold their breath and, through mirror neurons, channel your physiology to them. You give them cause to be concerned because they are also feeling the effects of fight-or-flight chemicals. By appropriately pausing, closing your mouth, and breathing, you encourage the audience to remain calm and receptive. They assign you credibility and perceive you as being intelligent and competent. As you become more conscious of your breathing and how it impacts others, you become a more effective presenter.

## Practice 1.5 | Establish Credibility

This rehearsal is designed to support your learning related to the skills of establishing credibility. To complete this rehearsal exercise, first think of an upcoming meeting, training, or other professional learning event where you are the presenter. In the left-hand column, write your verbal script to your opening. In the right-hand column, create your nonverbal choreography incorporating the five skills that support the establishing of credibility. Once you have completed your design, practice.

| Verbal Message | Nonverbal Choreography |
| --- | --- |
| | Voice |
| | Stance |
| | Pause |
| | Gesture |
| | Breathing |
| Example: | |
| Good morning, and thank you for the invitation to work with you today. | From center stage, stand still. And with a slight head tilt for approachability, using a credible voice and a palms-up gesture sweeping toward the group, say, "Good morning." Shift to approachable voice and say, "Thank you." Use a one-handed gesture (hand vertical), as you start to say, "Thank." Move the gesture downward and then freeze the gesture as you say, "You." Then use both hands to gesture to the group as you finish the statement. |

## THE RIFF OF COMMUNICATION

Whether or not you ever played guitar, you are probably familiar with the concept of a riff in music. It is the repeating harmonic pattern in a song or melody. For our purposes, we consider the patterns found in the 7 Essential Abilities to have RIFFs, characteristics of range, intensity, and frequency. These are also important aspects of nonverbal communication. Range is the quality related to how far away from baseline a pattern is deployed. For instance, a gesture

> **RIFF**
>
> *Range*—how far off your normal baseline
>
> *Intensity*—the sharpness and speed of the pattern when implemented
>
> *Frequency*—how many times a pattern is used in a given time period

may extend only to the point where the elbow is next to the torso, or it may extend to where the elbow is 10 or 12 inches from the torso. The further from the baseline level next to the torso, the larger the range.

Intensity is a quality related to the sharpness and speed with which a pattern is used. One way to understand intensity is to think of how people use gestures when speaking. In baseball, the umpire is the master of the dance. When he calls balls and strikes, the speed and sharpness of his gestures indicating balls and strikes contributes to the drama of the game. Sometimes a called strike comes slightly delayed after the ball reaches the catcher's glove and the umpire's hand comes up, slowly indicating a strike. At other times, as the ball enters the catcher's glove, the umpire quickly and sharply slices his arm down and up in a classic strike move—it is definitive, dramatic, and not up for negotiation.

Frequency refers to how often the pattern is used. Generally, the more frequently a pattern is used, the less effective it becomes.

To better understand range, think of variations in your own voice volume and pitch. In some settings, such as a lecture, you may speak more loudly than you would when sitting on the couch next to your spouse. Think also about how often you gesture, deliberately or habitually. There is great variation in the number of times a person gestures when speaking. Reflect on an emotional conversation. You may remember that you started that conversation using a quiet voice with few gestures. As emotions intensified, your voice very likely increased in pitch and volume. There was also a good chance that you increased the frequency and intensity of your gestures. Becoming aware of personal range and frequency helps you better choose specific nonverbal moves.

To increase your effectiveness as a presenter, it is a good idea to extend your range of voice tone and choose the appropriate tone depending on the intent. It is important when presenting to recognize that there will be times when use of the appropriate and specific tone will be outside your normal range at work or home. It isn't always as simple as choosing one or the other voice tone. Rather, it is a dynamic interplay between the two—using each with deliberate intention. Appropriate use of voice selection can increase a group's perception of your credibility as a presenter.

A dear friend who is a gifted presenter expertly uses humor in his presentations. He uses jokes for transition between different topics. After a joke, he switches to a credible stance so seamlessly that the audience knows by the modulation shift in his voice that he is now teaching content. The audience takes out their pencils, ready to take notes. A flattening of his voice tone as well as his shift in stance and gesture indicate the transition to the new content.

## SUMMARY

✓ Credibility is a presenter characteristic perceived and assigned by the group.

✓ Using the approachable voice, a presenter builds positive relationships that encourage participation by creating a psychologically safe environment with strong rapport.

✓ Congruent use of voice tone contributes to participants' perception of the presenter's credibility. The credible voice has a narrow range of tonal quality, and the chin often drops at the end of a phrase or sentence.

✓ Using the approachable voice, presenters build positive relationships that encourage participation by creating a psychological safe environment with strong rapport.

✓ Increasing the range of verbal and nonverbal skills offers greater potential for a presenter to have influence with the rich diversity of participants attending the session.

✓ The pause can be used to establish credibility because it can increase the group's perception of a presenter's intelligence, thoughtfulness, passion, and empathy.

✓ A still hand gesture is the visual correlation to an auditory pause.

✓ A presenter's breathing pattern absolutely influences how the audience breathes and thinks.

# 2 Build and Sustain Rapport

*Water is fluid, soft, and yielding. But water will wear away rock, which is rigid and cannot yield. As a rule, whatever is fluid, soft, and yielding will overcome whatever is rigid and hard. This is another paradox: what is soft is strong.*

Lao-Tzu

**R**apport is the dance in relationships that opens the door and invites learning. As important as it is to establish credibility, and it is important, we want to be mindful that if we as presenters stay within patterns that only convey credibility, it will become counterproductive to participants' learning. So the dance of rapport must begin early. Once credibility is established, the next goal is to build and sustain rapport. You establish credibility to appeal to the participants' intellectual curiosity about the presenter and the content, whereas you establish rapport to start building a relationship between yourself and the group in order to support participants' learning.

So what exactly is rapport? What does it look like? What does it sound like? How does it feel? Although it might be very difficult to describe or deconstruct, it is easy to identify. When you are a participant in a workshop or seminar, you absolutely know if and when the presenter has rapport with the participants. You can see rapport by how they are sitting, how they are breathing, and how they are interacting with the presenter and each other. We believe rapport can be consciously initiated and maintained by a presenter, and as a presenter you want to get prolific at using the skills that support rapport. That includes knowing the skills, understanding the context, and applying them across a range, intensity, and frequency.

> A successful learning experience is when your communication patterns are congruent with your intentions.

As you ease into the presentation, you build rapport to create a learning environment in which relationships contribute to the learning. It is not our contention that you should follow a rigid choreography, nor do we suggest it. We are adamant nonetheless that the dance steps followed in the first five minutes of any presentation are crucial and contribute significantly to the overall success of the session. Our intention is not to be inflexible; rather it is to be flexible and to access a deliberate framework of skills. Think of the tension between flexibility and inflexibility like the tension on a rope that is being pulled from two ends. At one end is the rigidity of the choreographed steps; at the other end, the rich dynamic and complex nuance of implementation—much like the tension between implementing academic standards while honoring academic freedom. What we do want is to be precise, accurate, and appropriate with the skills that contribute to rapport. The first five minutes of any presentation often determine whether you will be working from the first and 10 or the second and 25. A first down is still possible; it just requires a whole lot more footwork.

## WHY RAPPORT IS IMPORTANT— CAN'T THEY JUST LEARN IT?

You lay the groundwork for a successful learning experience when your communication patterns are congruent with your intentions, and rapport significantly contributes to participant learning. How important is rapport? Mast (2007) looked at physician-patient interaction and found that doctors with higher rapport significantly impacted patient satisfaction when compared to doctors who did not establish rapport. In a study by McCafferty (2004), it was found that the learning of English language learners was accelerated when they mirrored the nonverbal patterns of the teachers. The mirroring of gestures and other nonverbal patterns forms the foundation of rapport (Wells, 1999).

As a presenter, by increasing your own awareness, consciousness, and strategic implementation, you encourage participants to perceive you as knowledgeable in the content area as well as receptive and respectful of what they bring to the topic. So as a presenter, you absolutely want to be purposeful in your intent. You want to focus your attention on your intention. That intent is to establish an optimum learning environment high in rapport and cognitive challenge that accelerates and deepens learning. When there is rapport, participants feel psychologically safe yet cognitively responsive. They are fully present, open, and receptive. That state of mind makes it possible for them to find value. As a presenter, you can enhance participants' learning by being more aware of your intent so that you can be deliberate and skillful with the communication patterns that establish and maintain rapport.

Having an understanding of human physiology helps you determine your options and guide your choices. When making a presentation to a group of people, chances are good that you are introducing something new or different to them. Whether it is a new concept, innovation, or protocol is of little consequence. The very fact that it differs from the status quo can cause participants to be resistant and defensive. The probability of defensiveness and all the accompanying physiological changes gets ratcheted up when it is a forced march. Looking at the initiatives and research in education from the past 20 years, it is inevitable that as a presenter you will be delivering a change initiative message to some participants who are defensive or resistant. Recognizing this self-evident truth allows you to be proactive and strategic in reframing the message in order to respectfully support the learning of this type of tough crowd.

## RAPPORT REROUTES THREAT RESPONSES

Humans are hardwired to protect themselves from outside threats, whether they are actual or perceived assaults or insults. Emotional threats in the absence of rapport run the risk of initiating the release of cortisol, and this hormone makes it more difficult to engage the higher-level thinking skills. Emotional threat in the absence of rapport results in cognitive dissonance. In fact, looking at MRI results, Westen, Blagov, Harenski, Kilts, and Hamann (2006) found that the mere fact of listening to someone who holds a different point of view from our own causes decreased activity in the thinking part of our brain. It is our contention that establishing rapport prior to introducing ideas that may challenge participants is critical to fending off the type of cognitive dissonance that limits thinking. Knowing this, one of our objectives is to choreograph the steps of rapport and lead the dance partner to a state low in emotional threat and high in cognitive responsiveness. In this state, the door of consideration is wide open.

Creating the psychological safety for real learning requires a carefully choreographed dance in the pursuit of rapport. When this is executed skillfully, participants are more willing to follow the presenter's lead while feeling safe enough to risk cognitive vulnerability and the examination of deeply held assumptions and beliefs. Having been participants in a respectful learning environment, they leave the presentation different in skill, knowledge, or disposition because they accepted the invitation to examine their thinking and consider different possibilities. Thoughtful design and a respectful learning environment make that possible. And the first step in that journey is rapport.

Rapport is a short-term psychological state in which the lines of communication are wide open. The people involved have nearly all of their conscious thought processes focused on what is being said and what they have to say. They are open to considering the information being presented and are not defensive.

## BLINK. THERE GOES RAPPORT

"With all due respect, I disagree with your idea. I think . . ."

The presenter listens to the participant's comment and intellectual challenge and then says, "Isn't that an interesting idea? But I think . . ."

Our hunch is that many of us have been participants in a presentation during which someone put forward an idea or question only to be shot down by the presenter. It does not take the group long to recognize that they are not in a safe learning environment. The likelihood that learning will take place becomes obstructed as the incoming data seems to threaten what they know or believe. Survival is the brain's primary function. We are hardwired to then become defensive and are less able to process with an open mind. Regardless of whether the information might help us do our jobs better, we switch into our protective mode and defend our current practices and beliefs. As Carl Glickman (1998) tells us, without the will to change there can be no change. Rapport is essential for change.

When you have rapport with a group, there is a harmonious connection. It is an essential ingredient in building a climate of trust. We agree with Art Costa and Bob Garmston (2002) that "you can draw on specific verbal and nonverbal behavior to nurture the relationship" (p. 77). While trust usually happens over a longer period of time, rapport happens in the moment. It is the cornerstone of learning because it is through rapport that you establish the open psychological pathways that allow participants to even consider ideas different from their own.

## I HEAR YOU

*The colossal misunderstanding of our time is the assumption that insight will work with people who are unmotivated to change.*

*Communication does not depend on syntax, or eloquence, or rhetoric, or articulation but on the emotional context in which the message is being heard. People can only hear you when they are moving toward you, and they are not likely to when your words are pursuing them. Even the choicest words lose their power when they are used to overpower. Attitudes are the real figures of speech.*

Edwin H. Friedman

❖

## RESISTANCE IS FUTILE

It was about an hour into a two-day session focusing on ways to attract more men into the teaching profession. The presenter asked the group to surface their thinking as to reasons why men might not be choosing teaching as a profession. One participant, using a credible voice accompanied by a high breathing pattern, said, "Who the heck would want to become a teacher? There aren't enough books for every student. There is no money for professional development. Class sizes are too large!" His nonverbals were easy to read. He was emotionally on high alert. Upon hearing this, the presenter made a deliberate and strategic move that began with one small step away from the location where she was standing when the comment was made. Using the same voice tone, pace of speech, breathing pattern, and emotional energy as the participant, she said, "As a committed educator, the lack of resources becomes frustrating." She paused with a palm up gesture in the direction of the participant, who said, "Absolutely!" and he breathed. The presenter breathed calmly and in an approachable voice said, "And that is the reason we are asking these questions; we want to make teaching as fulfilling a profession as it can be." While the presenter made this statement, the participant continued to breathe calmly and for the remainder of the day was an attentive, engaged, and positive contributor. He did not breathe high at any time during the rest of the day.

❖

This dance was deliberate. The presenter recognized the downshift and matched the participant's nonverbal patterns. Once the participant acknowledged that he was heard, the presenter shifted to an approachable pattern. Because they were in rapport, she was able to short-circuit the downshifting pathway and bring the participant into a more constructive state that led to the generation of ideas as opposed to a litany of complaints.

## THE NEURO CONNECTION

In Chapter 1 we discussed mirror neurons and their connection to breathing. It turns out that these same premotor neurons are tightly linked to empathy and rapport. Psychologists have pondered for years why humans have the capacity to feel bad when someone else feels bad. Recent research reported by Ginot (2009) links mirror neurons to "how people 'get' the emotional states and behavioral intentions of others" (p. 8).

Watching sports on TV is another excellent example of mirror neuron systems in action. Think about it: you are sitting in your den, watching a game—only watching. When a great play happens for the team you are rooting for, good feelings. When the advantage goes the other way, feelings of defeat, frustration, or sadness. Why? In one sense, it makes no sense. You are not playing the game; you are not there; you are not part of the live audience. Yet you feel as they do. Mirror neurons provide an intriguing explanation for this behavior.

Taking this a step further, if you know that humans have mirror neuron systems and you know that consciousness is not necessary to activate the system, then as an effective presenter you can tap into the mirror neuron system of participants. Having rapport is the observable data indicating that the mirror neuron complex may be stimulated. By tapping into participants' mirror systems, you can increase their positive emotional connection to the content, to each other, and to you.

## RAPPORT OPENS THINKING

Goleman (2006) tells us that rapport and empathy are expressed nonverbally. And Rosenthal, Hall, DiMatteo, Rogers, and Archer (1979) have found that rapport always entails three elements: shared positive feelings, mutual attention, and a well-coordinated nonverbal duet. As these three arise in tandem, rapport is catalyzed, and there are patterns you can adopt to make this happen (mirroring breathing, gestures, voice tone, energy, etc.). "Rapport is so thick that their [both parties involved in the communication] posture and movements mirror each other as though intentionally choreographed" (Goleman, 2006, p. 27). Furthermore, in *Gesture: Visible Action as Utterance,* Kendon (2004) describes the importance of gesture in the development of rapport and the contribution to learning.

---

## SURFACING RESISTANCE

A session is just under way, and the presenter concludes her impact statement; credibility has been established. She takes a step to the side and, with more modulation in her voice and a slightly tilted head, begins to outline the structure of the day, identifying break times, ending times, and other housekeeping details. She notices more relaxed breathing, more fluidity in the movements of the participants. As she states the presentation outcomes using a credible voice and then nods with affirmation, the group nods with her. Using an approachable voice and a new location, she begins, "Given these outcomes," as she points and looks at the visual display. She turns to the group while extending a sweeping and curved, palm-up hand gesture and, in an approachable voice, continues, "What might be some of your expectations during our three days together?" Pausing briefly, she continues in an approachable voice, "Please," then shifts to a credible voice and says, "share with a neighbor." Without hesitation, participants turn and engage with their partner. After about two minutes the presenter, now standing next to the easel, brings the group back from their activity and, using an approachable voice and inviting gesture, says, "Let's hear some of your expectations." As the silent pause fills the room and the palm-up gesture invites participants to share, hands rise and participants willingly voice their expectations.

One participant says, "I want to be able to learn some skills I can use right away." The presenter, standing still, head gently tilted and maintaining direct eye contact with the speaker, continues to be silent a moment after the participant completes the statement. Using a palm-up gesture and holding a hand in a curved pose, the presenter paraphrases the comment and says, "So, you want concrete skills that you can apply in your classroom." The participant says, "Yes!" and the presenter writes "Concrete and applicable skills" on the easel.

---

This presenter engaged in an intentionally choreographed dance. The dance began and connections were started between the presenter and the group. There are deliberate moves and communication patterns that help to establish rapport. The intention is to support learning. You want participants to be open to new learning and be comfortable (but not too comfortable—more on that later) with you as the presenter, with the group, and with the content. There are various ways to create one-on-one rapport as well as group rapport. It can happen naturally and be established very quickly if you listen attentively to the audience and pay close attention to your verbal and nonverbal communication. When people are communicating well, they are relaxed, comfortable, and in alignment. There is a parallel in voice tone, language, gesture, stance, and breathing. Mirroring or matching is how you offer back without attaching any judgment to what you say or do.

## USING RAPPORT TO NEUTRALIZE RESISTANCE

Our experience with groups has taught us that if we do not ask a contentious group how they feel about attending the presentation or their relationship to the content, they will make their feelings known through behaviors that are counterproductive to learning. Consider Claudette's story from a session with district leaders.

### REFRAMING RESISTANCE

I was tasked with working with a group of district curriculum coordinators to start planning for the implementation of a mandated professional learning program. As I walked into the room, one of the coordinators was sitting in the chair that was reserved for the presenter, me. His arms were tightly crossed, and he glared at me as I walked in. His posture and breathing were clear indicators that said, "You are not welcome here." In fact, the rest of the people in the room appeared to mirror the same sentiment; it was pervasive. In short, I was there to tell them what they needed to do to be in compliance, and they were there because they had to be. Resistance is easily recognized in a captive audience.

Recognizing the intense resistance, I knew my original opening would not be effective with this group, so it was put on hold. Instead, I decided to open with a question. Striking an approachable stance, with my head tilted significantly and my shoulders raised, I also raised my hand and said, "Who here feels they have more work than time to do it?" Several hands tentatively emerged. "And that may very well be true in the short run; however, what we found is that once this program is implemented it builds capabilities and capacity. That makes our jobs easier. As you think about that, what are some of your thoughts about being here today?"

Time and space were given for each participant to respond. Tensions eased, bodies relaxed, breathing calmed some. Once all the participants had had a chance to verbalize their feelings, they were more present in the moment and more open to hearing the message.

So what was delivered beyond the verbal message? First, remember that Claudette's intention was to get the group to shift from feeling nonreceptive and resistant to being at least willing to listen. Prior to the beginning of the opening statement, she was in a credible stance. As the opening statement began, she shifted to an approachable stance and then raised her hand as she said, "Who here. . . ." Some participants raised their hands, others nodded, and some even answered affirmatively. As Claudette said, "And that may very well be true . . ." she was already in a different location, just a step or two from the initial location, and her voice continued in an approachable tone. After a three-second pause at the end of that phrase, she began the next statement using a voice of passion. The voice of passion includes a whisper with a pace of speech slightly slower than the previous statements. Her palms were facing upward as she concluded the statement. She paused and took a step back toward, but not all the way back to the initial location, and said in an approachable voice, "As you think about that. . . ." Within seconds, several participants took deep breaths and appeared to shift to a more relaxed and attentive posture. Their feelings of frustration were acknowledged, and both individually and as a group they started breathing more slowly, their pace of speech slowed, and they even looked at the presenter. And as the group voiced their feelings, the group shifted to an increasingly calm disposition.

It is often believed that to be in rapport, there must be agreement. The real beauty of rapport is that sharing others' views is not at all a prerequisite. What is needed is a sense of being open to and respectful of their thinking. It is a question of both receiving and offering information without attaching judgment. In the previous story, Claudette did not necessarily agree with the participants, but she did hear and could understand their frame of reference and she also acknowledged their perceptions. By doing that, the stage was set for rapport building. "Set" in the sense that the group had shifted from high alert, high threat with a hijacked amygdala to a state in which their thinking could be accessed. The learning environment was prepped for putting ideas on the table in a way that allows people to consider those ideas even when they are different from their own. An initial step for developing rapport with others is listening to hear, not to speak. The next step is to let them know they are heard and understood. It is much more likely that people will listen once they sense they have been heard.

## THERE IS SOMETHING COMING

We all know that on traffic signals a green light follows a red light. Imagine what driving would be like if the traffic lights changed from green to red with no yellow light. How comfortable would approaching an intersection like that be for you? As a conscientious driver approaching the intersection, you would probably become tense from the anticipation of the immediate signal change. If the light changed from green to red with no yellow, your arms and legs would tense up as you slammed on your brakes, and, rest assured, you would stop breathing. Additionally, if you were in a conversation with the person next to you, there is a good chance that as the light changed and you hit the breaks, you would also stop talking and all thoughts about that conversation would leave your mind. The freeze in thought while driving is similar to the neurological and physiological response you have when there is no foreshadowing in a training environment.

Imagine what an all-day workshop would look like without a yellow light to foreshadow what was coming. What might you feel or think? Without foreshadowing, there is a good chance that any rapport between the presenter and the group would be lost when whatever was approaching arrived without warning, as in the following example.

Have you ever attended a session at which a presenter said, "Are there any questions?" and no one asked any questions? Not even you, even though you had a question? If this is an experience you have had, our hunch is that there was no foreshadowing. If the presenter had only said, "In about 10 minutes, after we finish this segment, there will be an opportunity to ask some questions. You may already have some, so jot them down in your notes and we will address them soon." Foreshadowing using a yellow light like this often results in a tide of questions and comments.

Foreshadowing can be effectively used at the onset of any training to let people know how they may feel throughout the day. Knowing that some adults feel uncomfortable practicing in front of their peers, we consistently let participants know that they might feel uncomfortable at times because we offer the opportunity to practice and rehearse. This foreshadowing is done not to prevent or circumvent their discomfort; rather, it is done to let them know how they might feel so that when they do feel that way they have anticipated it and can continue to learn and not downshift. We also foreshadow this bit of discomfort to let them know that if they are feeling that way, they are in fact learning.

## THE BLACK DIAMOND LEARNING ZONE

I (Claudette) and my family look forward to our annual ski holiday. Each year my brother-in-law inquires about how well the sisters skied each day. For years I would say, "Great!" One year he asked, "What's your criterion for great?" That's when I realized my criteria for doing well was that none of us had fallen, which meant we had not really pushed

> We want to create a zone of disequilibrium that is uncomfortable enough to catalyze learning while emotionally safe enough to prevent downshifting.

ourselves from year to year. We were destined to forever be intermediate skiers mastering the blue hills. So to improve in my sport, I had to push myself onto a black diamond. I had to get out of my comfort zone and into my learning zone. And I improved. Did I feel uncomfortable as I was learning? Absolutely! As we know from Vygotsky (1978) and Piaget (1963), we have both a comfort zone and a learning zone. There is disequilibrium as we learn new concepts and skills, and that makes us feel a little uncomfortable. And unless we feel comfortable enough to feel uncomfortable, we won't learn. This is why rapport is so important.

Why is this important? Because using a foreshadowing technique supports rapport by not surprising people when shifts happen. If people are feeling comfortable through the whole presentation, then according to Piaget (1963) and Vygotsky (1978) they are not learning anything new. We want to create a zone of disequilibrium that is uncomfortable enough to catalyze learning while emotionally safe enough to prevent downshifting.

---

| Practice 2.1 | Foreshadowing |
| --- | --- |

Think of an upcoming training situation that you are responsible for planning. Next, identify two points in the training where you want the following to occur:

1. Participants will share their thinking.
2. You will let participants know they will be doing some hard thinking.

Create a narrative and choreography that serve as foreshadowing while maintaining rapport.

---

## RESISTANCE AND RAPPORT

Educators do not have enough time during the day to get done what they already have to do. It is inevitable that as a presenter you will encounter some resistance when presenting something new that the audience perceives as training for an add-on program. One of the most effective ways to encourage people to breathe and let go of some of their resistance is by simply acknowledging it. By acknowledging their resistance, you let them know that you have considered their different perspectives and understand them. This requires some specific choreography so that you can put the resistance out *there* and not have it stick to you. So what you say and how you say it are of equal importance.

To completely understand and successfully implement the dance that acknowledges resistance, you must first explore four communication points of reference. These are physical points of reference drawn from the works of

Grinder and Poyatos. *One-point* communication is when you, the presenter, refer to yourself. This can be done by gesturing toward yourself. *Two-point* communication is between you and a participant, table group, or whole group. *Third-point* communication is toward an object in the room, perhaps an easel, the screen, or participant work. The third point is inanimate and present in the room. *Fourth-point* communication is to a person, place, event, or thing not present in the room. As you will discover in Table 2.1 and Practice 2.2, the fourth point is used to name the resistance, thus assigning to someone or something other than the group. This move contributes to creating psychological safety and maintaining rapport with the group.

The script and choreography in Table 2.1 describes one way to acknowledge resistance. Read the verbal and nonverbal components, and then complete Practice 2.2.

**Table 2.1** Anticipating Resistance: Choreographing an Opening

| Verbal | Nonverbal |
|---|---|
| Thank you for coming this morning. | Maintain direct eye contact with group. Use a mix of credible and approachable voice with an open, palm-up gesture. |
| As if you had a choice! | Pause with the hands vertical. Stand still and wait for a laugh. |
| On the agenda are four topics . . . | Look at agenda, use a credible voice, pause after each topic. With the last topic stated, turn to the group, freeze your body, and count internally, 3-2-1. |
| Before we get started . . . | Silently walk a few feet from the easel (facilitation space). |
| I imagine a number of you would rather be _____ today and are resistant to being required to attend this workshop. | Gesture to the fourth point. Pause periodically. Use credible voice. At the end, stand still, pause, and silently count 3-2-1. Then move halfway back to the easel. |
| There is good reason to want to be with your students. For those of us in education, that is where our passion lies. | Speak in an approachable voice. Use a palm-up gesture to group and inclusive language (*our*). |
| Sometimes in order to serve our students well, we have to take care of our own learning. | Take a few steps toward the front center of the group. Speak in an approachable voice and use gestures of inclusion, palms up. Use downward beat gestures accompanying the words of your message like a maestro directing an orchestra. Pause, stand still, and silently count 3-2-1. |
| Our first agenda item is . . . (And get started) | Turn and walk toward the easel. Point to the first agenda item using a new voice pattern, pace, and volume as you state the first agenda item. |

---

**Practice 2.2** | **Acknowledging Resistance**

For an upcoming training, take a few moments to think about possible sources of resistance. Name the resistance in the space below.


Next, craft a narrative and design the choreography to identify and deliver the message to your group. Consider using Table 2.1 to facilitate your thinking, and then practice the dance.

---

## WHAT RAPPORT SOUNDS LIKE

When you are leading a workshop or meeting, rapport can be somewhat trickier to hear because there are so many voices in the room. One way to hear it is to listen for matches in language styles. By "language styles," we are referring to the types of verbs, adjectives, and nouns used when someone speaks. Table 2.2 lists over 100 words and organizes them according to sensory modality: visual, auditory, kinesthetic, and digital. Words in the digital category can be thought of as those with no sensory connection; in a sense they are "sense-less." The digital category is most easily recognized by thinking about bureaucratic speak. For instance, pick four or more of these words and make a sentence (e.g., "The proposal is *excellent* at *modeling* an *optimum* yet *integrated paradigm* with *variable systemic* applications").

The key to finding Table 2.2 useful is to first listen to participants speak and hear their sensory modality language. Then to help maintain rapport, use language from the same modality category when talking with them. We have found that when you speak using the same modality, there is greater fluidity to the conversation and a more open sharing of ideas.

**Table 2.2** Sensory Modalities

| Visual | Auditory | Kinesthetic | Digital |
|---|---|---|---|
| see | hear | feel | think |
| view | listen | grab | procedure |
| insight | sound | pull | tendency |
| reflection | tone | grasp | knowledge |
| watch | accent | rub | model |

*(Continued)*

(Continued)

| Visual | Auditory | Kinesthetic | Digital |
|---|---|---|---|
| show | musical | sticky | theory |
| look | call | get hold of | principle |
| picture | tune out | wrestle | meaning |
| focus | jingle | warm | know |
| scan | say | touch | specific |
| appear | click | pressure | interesting |
| reveal | resonate | handle | obvious |
| hazy | rhythm | texture | random |
| misty | harmony | heavy | special |
| observe | clash | firm | typical |
| image | speak | slip through | usual |
| glow | amplify | catch | excellent |
| brilliant | dialogue | slimy | basic |
| vivid | ring | smooth | understand |
| shine | chime | gritty | integrated |
| dim | discord | pushy | incremental |
| flash | noise | sting | enhanced |
| sparkle | quiet | contact | systematic |
| highlight | melody | itchy | optimal |
| bright | buzz | concrete | compatible |
| transparent | shout | wobble | paradigm |
| opaque | announce | snag | contingency |
| mirror | mute | solid | idea |
| snapshot | loud | tight | interactive |
| see | whisper | soft | balance |
|  |  | tough | variable |
|  |  | sharp | experience |

## Practice 2.3 | Matching Language

Read the following statements and questions. Decide whether the statement is visual, auditory, kinesthetic, or digital. For each question, construct an answer or paraphrase. Suggested responses are in italics.

1. It seems to me the additional work you are asking us to do will really bog us down and force us to wrestle with time management as well as struggle with balancing everything we have to do in a work day. *For you, the additional work may pull you in different directions and put pressure on your time?*

2. It would be more useful for me to have a snapshot from each part of the program so I can see the whole picture at one time while still seeing the individual frames. *So clarity for you is being able to see individual pictures within a panorama?*

3. How does that theory model effective teaching and integrate best practices in a way that is coordinated and systematic? *Specifically, you want to know how to achieve effective teaching through best practices?*

4. If we are not careful, students could slip through the cracks and we would be unable to help them grasp the content standards in time. *As we grapple with this issue, in what ways might we catch the students who are falling?*

5. This new program is interesting although not compatible with the current paradigm. *In what ways do you consider it interesting?*

6. It appears we will gain some insight into student understanding with this new program. *As we focus on student understanding, how might the information brighten our views?*

7. We need to dialogue. *You're suggesting an additional conversation?*

8. I'm wrestling with it. *Does anything feel useful to you?*

9. Wow, this resonates with me. *Tell me specifically, what sounds useful to you?*

10. It is obvious that the new integrated, systematic model will optimize a balanced procedure. *Obvious in what three or four basic and specific ways?*

11. I'd like to share the interesting ideas that teachers typically experienced during the pilot program. *What new knowledge enhanced your experience?*

12. I'd like to highlight some of the insights that appeared during the pilot program. *Tell us what appeared to be the most vivid outcome for you.*

13. I'd like to announce what resonated with the teachers during the pilot program. *Let's hear what you have to accent—the buzz about the new program is exciting.*

14. I'd like to capture what the teachers got a handle on during the pilot program. *I'd like to capture your feelings on the firm benefits of this program.*

Key

| Statement/Question | V | A | K | D |
|:---:|:---:|:---:|:---:|:---:|
| 1 | | | X | |
| 2 | X | | | |
| 3 | | | | X |
| 4 | | | X | |
| 5 | | | | X |
| 6 | X | | | |
| 7 | | X | | |
| 8 | | | X | |
| 9 | | X | | |
| 10 | | | | X |
| 11 | | | | X |
| 12 | X | | | |
| 13 | | X | | |
| 14 | | | X | |

In addition to recognizing and matching sensory language, another useful model for revealing how a person is thinking comes from Dilts with collaboration by Gumm (see Gumm, Walker, & Day, 1982). This model relies on eye patterns (see Figure 2.1) to access learning modalities and is a good indicator of Dunn and Griggs's (1988) VAK (visual-auditory-kinesthetic) model that so many educators are familiar with. We caution that eye patterns alone should not be the only source for determining someone's style. Using eye patterns along with word selection and body

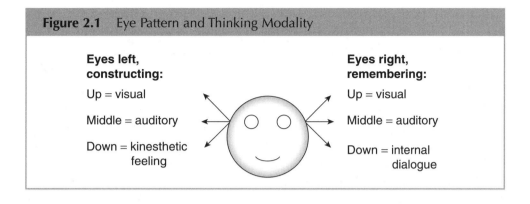

**Figure 2.1** Eye Pattern and Thinking Modality

**Eyes left, constructing:**

Up = visual

Middle = auditory

Down = kinesthetic feeling

**Eyes right, remembering:**

Up = visual

Middle = auditory

Down = internal dialogue

movements provides valuable data for a presenter who wants to establish and maintain rapport as well as support adult learning.

This model of accessing eye patterns can be useful when presenting because accessing eye patterns can be a view into how people are thinking, much the same way that gestures give a more complete understanding than words alone. For example, a participant asks you a question and uses kinesthetic language such as, "I have been wrestling with that concept for some time, and nothing seems to hit me with any concrete applications." You might reply, "What if anything feels more firm or seems to make an impact on your thinking?" Then watch. As the participant thinks, and if he is congruent, you should see him look down while thinking and forming his response. This can confirm his preferred thinking modality in the moment. By knowing his preferred thinking modality (in this case kinesthetic), you can maintain rapport with him by staying in a kinesthetic dialogue as long as he continues to do so.

## WHAT RAPPORT LOOKS LIKE

Sit in any restaurant and discreetly look around the room. You can see when people are in or out of rapport just by observing their nonverbal patterns. If they are in sync, we say they are in high rapport. If they are out of sync, we say rapport is missing or low. What does in sync look like? In a sense, it looks like a reflection in the mirror. This transient, subtle, yet powerful skill of rapport is a mirroring of the physical characteristics of the person or group you are communicating with.

One-on-one rapport is easier than group rapport because you only have to match one person. We will continue to explain rapport from a one-on-one perspective and extend the learning to the whole group by the end of the chapter. As you will discover, the patterns of rapport are the same in any setting; the difference between one-on-one and group rapport has to do with perception and where you, as a presenter, look to access the data informing you when you have group rapport and when you lose it.

The challenge in mirroring body movements to gain rapport lies in the subtle difference between mirroring and parroting. When done well, mirroring results in an increase in receptivity, openness, a sense of trust, and a sense of being listened to and understood. Parroting, on the other hand, comes across as offensive, condescending, satirical, and many other negative perceptions. So what is the difference between parroting and mirroring?

A short answer is that parroting is an immediate and exact match in word, tone, breathing, and gesture. Mirroring is more of a reflection, and it is delayed by about three seconds. No matter how good the mirror, reflections are not perfect images of the original. Think about physical mirrors—there are distortions as a result of imperfections in the glass, and the angle of the reflection is different from the angle of the source of the image. Interestingly, a reflection is also opposite the original. Just think about reading the word *ambulance* in your rearview mirror and then turning around to face it, only to find that it is backwards. These subtle differences are enough to make a huge difference in rapport when communicating.

Gaining rapport takes practice. It is not perfect every time, and it can be lost in a heartbeat. Losing rapport can result from something you did or from an external source in the room, like the sound of a door opening, a phone ringing, or something as simple as a third person interrupting or joining the conversation. Because rapport is ephemeral and in some cases almost elusive, we recommend practicing in a safe and welcoming environment.

One place that is great for practicing rapport is in a restaurant because the livelihood of the server depends on her ability to establish rapport.

### HARBOR RAPPORT

Last spring, in a restaurant in Boothbay Harbor, Maine, I (Kendall) went with a group of about eight Mainers, all professional developers and leaders in mathematics education, to a restaurant. We took a seat at a rectangular table, and the waitress walked up and asked if we wanted drinks. A few folks hemmed and hawed. The waitress abruptly said, "I'll come back in a few minutes." Her response was out of sync with the group, who perceived that she was being rude by being abrupt. Of course, we must remember reality is what you perceive and not what you intend. The server most likely did not intend to offend; however, at our table that was the perception.

When the server returned, she began taking drink orders. Since we had just came out of a full-day session on nonverbal patterns, one of the participants at the table decided to establish rapport and try to get the waitress to shift her breathing—to lighten up. To do that, when the waitress got to him, he paused and asked her a question about the menu using the same abrupt language pattern she was using. She responded back, mirroring him. Then he shifted his pattern by turning to look at her and saying in an approachable voice, "You know, you would know best between the crab cakes and the clam chowder. . . ." Before I tell you what happened next, it is important to know that this was a conscious and deliberate act on the part of the person asking the question. His intention was to get the other person to shift and follow his lead, which is one characteristic of rapport; specifically, it is rapport not only when we match but also when we lead and have the other person follow our nonverbal pattern.

❖

So what happened? The server shifted to the level of friendliness we had when we first walked in. Upon hearing the comment and implied question, she let out a little humble aside statement, paused, took a deep breath, and then matched the same approachable voice and gestures used to ask the question. As she continued taking orders around the table, that same welcoming, humorous, and delightful personality remained.

Let's think of a whole group and what rapport looks like. In the *Elusive Obvious*, Grinder (2008) explains that group rapport is recognized when a group responds to the presenter in unison. For instance, the presenter may tell a joke and everyone laughs at the same time. Or the presenter may effectively use a third point and everyone looks at the third point at the same time. Grinder suggests that any time the entire group does something at the same time, there is high group rapport.

Since many of the readers of this book were or are teachers, you may be thinking, "Yeah, right. Get a whole group to do something at the same time? Try teaching third grade, seventh grade, twelfth grade, heck any grade, and see if you can get everyone to do something at the same time."

Yes, that is a great challenge indeed. Getting a group to do something at the same time takes training, so why not train the group using an indirect approach? By "indirect" we mean don't tell the group you are training them; just go ahead and do it. An example is one we often use at the beginning of our workshops, and many gifted presenters use a similar strategy. Our purposes for using this strategy, "Like Me," include establishing group rapport and assessing the group's experience, interests, and connections to the work into which we are about to venture.

Since one purpose for this activity is group rapport, evidence of rapport will be synchronicity. You can have individuals in the group stand when the "like me" statement applies to them. For instance, in a group of teachers you might say, "I am a teacher with 5 to 10 years of experience." Those who recognize themselves in that statement stand and say, "Like me." It is most effective to make several statements, including some with humor if it fits your personality. The key is to orchestrate it so that those who fit the description respond in unison.

Another skill for establishing group rapport is related to unison of response. In this instance, we refer to releasing the group to do an activity. Generally, it is fairly safe to assume that at the beginning of any workshop, group safety is not as high as it will be once the group is formed. Adult groups pose several challenges in professional workplace learning environments, one of which is related to creating enough safety in the room so that adults willingly share their learning with a colleague, table group, or whole group. This type of rapport building takes practice and time.

There are specific strategies you can use to be more effective at establishing rapport with adult groups. In a learning environment, it is generally considered more psychologically safe to share an idea with one person than to share that idea with three or four people or an entire group. So to build positive group rapport, consider having some of the first participant interactions in groups of two. As the smoothness in transitions increases from pairs to whole group, slowly move the group to work in trios and fours.

When debriefing the activity—whether in pairs, trios, fours, or whole table—to increase the safety and maintain rapport, keep the question source ambiguous. For instance, when asking a question, instead of asking, "What do you think about . . ." ask "What did you and your partner discuss about. . . ." By increasing the distance between the source and the answer, ambiguity remains and psychological safety is ensured. As the answer is shared, whether right or wrong, the groups' reaction is to the response and not the person. There is no judgment made about the person. Orchestrating well-crafted questions ensures safety for participants and is a strong and useful skill for maintaining group rapport.

We cannot overemphasize the importance of crafting and implementing good questions that promote psychological safety and push cognitive challenge. In all adult learning situations, there is a broad range of knowledge, experience, and ego. How many staff meetings have you attended where territory is secured and boundaries defined? We had a delightful staff at a school where I (Kendall) once worked. The staff had high rapport with each other and low rapport with the principal. Every staff meeting had similar patterns. An agenda was read, a topic raised, and then . . . like clockwork . . . a hand would come up from one of the faculty. Using a credible voice, stiff gestures, and direct eye contact, the challenge was laid down. The principal would vent steam out his ears, and the staff would sit still with a sense of shock. The principal and teacher would exchange statements for about five minutes as the rest of the staff sat silently. Eventually the principal or staff member would say, "We can talk later" or "I disagree, let's just continue with the agenda."

## WHAT RAPPORT FEELS LIKE

When you are in rapport with another person or with a group, you feel connected. All of your energy is centered on the interaction that is taking place. All the surrounding stimuli are blocked out, and you are not searching for what to say. The conversation flows, and there are no pregnant pauses.

### PHONY RAPPORT

I (Claudette) was talking with my sister on the phone. Because we live some 3,000 miles apart, phone conversations are our most common form of communication. In this conversation, she was talking about a situation she was having at work. It was making her uncomfortable, and she wanted to figure out what to do and what I thought about the situation.

After a few minutes of listening, I paraphrased and asked a probing question. I was really beginning to understand her situation, and she was becoming very clear in the direction she wanted to take. I was sitting near my computer as we were talking, not using it, just sitting near it. However, as we were talking, out of the corner of my eye I noticed an e-mail notification. The message was from a client, and I urgently needed to read it because of a particular time crunch we were experiencing. So I opened the e-mail and read it.

Before I got two sentences in, my sister said in a stern yet violated voice, "What are you doing? Are you reading e-mail?" What was I to do or say? I broke rapport and it was obvious—she knew I was no longer listening, no longer receptive to receiving the message. As humans, we intuitively and immediately know when rapport is broken, even at a distance of a few thousand miles.

We know the feeling of no rapport—it is distant and cold; there is little emotional connection or commitment. When we are in rapport, we are closer, more connected, and our emotions related to friendship, trust, and caring are activated. Why is so much chemistry and physiology influenced by rapport? The answer may surprise you.

## ROAMING THE ROOM

When participants are engaged in table group activities, the opportunity to roam the room provides the presenter with time to establish (and practice) rapport with table groups and individuals. The following scenario is offered to provide an example of how to approach someone who may not be in rapport with you, may not even want to be present in the session. By studying this scenario you may develop the ability to recognize resistance and learn a few patterns that can make a difference in reaching the difficult-to-reach adult participants.

### WHEN RAPPORT MAY BE TOUGH TO ESTABLISH

About an hour into a daylong session, you continue to notice one participant. He appears to make less direct eye contact with you than most others in the audience. He often side talks and appears thus far to superficially engage with the activities. Your sense at this time is that he is not strongly connected to the content, and in fact his behavior appears to be interfering with others at the table who are trying to participate. While presenting some content and setting up the next activity, you decide you will pay him a visit during the next table group activity.

You release participants into the activity and slowly make your way toward him. You approach in a way that he can notice you in his peripheral vision. As you approach his table, your eyes are on his notebook and you scan the table. Using a low-volume credible voice you ask, "So what are you thinking?" This question is delightfully ambiguous in that it asks what he is thinking but not about the subject, thus leaving it completely open for him to comment on something personal or related to the session content. The question also has a positive presupposition that he is in fact thinking. A positive presupposition in a question contributes to a more welcoming perception as opposed to a perception of being challenged or interrogated.

His response is a little aloof: "Not much."

Your response is a paraphrase and probe. "So there is not much here for you or . . . [pause], I've noticed you for a while and was wondering if today's topic [looking at the workbook] is of value to you?" Then you look at him. As he responds, he slowly turns toward you. As he does, you look back at the work and listen to his response. If rapport is beginning, he will look to where you are looking. If this happens, then look back at him. If rapport is building, he will then look at you. As he turns, look back at the paper. This rapport-establishing skill is called *leading,* and it occurs when your patterns are mirrored by the other person's patterns. Once leading is successful, you can reduce it and begin mirroring him.

During his response, he reveals that he has done some of this before, did not find it useful then, and feels it will not be useful now. What a great opportunity to strengthen rapport. As he finishes his comment you say, "Thank you." Then, gesturing toward him with a palm up and moving the gesture toward you, you say, "So you feel this may be a waste of your time. I felt the same way the first time I saw this [now switch your gesture to point toward the booklet and look toward the booklet] assessment program. What I found [gesture to yourself and look back at him] was that once we debriefed and evaluated our lessons, the modifications we made resulted in a huge difference in student achievement. It made a real difference."

The next step is to get a commitment from him. Consider asking, "As we continue looking at this program [look at the booklet and gesture toward the booklet, pause, then turn to him and gesture from him to you with a palm-up gesture, and use an approachable voice], let me know when you see something useful or hear an idea that resonates for you or think of a move that will tackle some of your challenges." This final statement is a VAK question. With careful observation skills, you will notice which phrase he responds to. It will be either visual, auditory, or kinesthetic. By recognizing where he is in the moment, when you return to presenting to the whole group, you can insert verbs supporting his modality. If you established rapport successfully, you will see a positive shift in his attention.

List three ideas you find important to remember from this scenario.

1.

2.

3.

List two skills you want to remember from this scenario.

1.

2.

❖

## SUMMARY

✓ Creating the psychological safety to support real learning requires a carefully choreographed dance in the pursuit of rapport.

✓ When people are communicating well, they are relaxed, comfortable, and in alignment. There is a parallel in voice tone, language, gesture, stance, and breathing. Mirroring or matching is how you offer back without attaching judgment to what you say or do.

✓ It is often believed that to be in rapport, there must be agreement. The real beauty of rapport is that sharing others' views is not at all a prerequisite. What is needed is a sense of being open to and respectful of their thinking.

✓ Foreshadowing using a yellow light (to use a traffic light metaphor) can be effectively used at the onset of any training to let people know how they may feel throughout the day. The foreshadowing is done not to prevent or circumvent their discomfort; rather, it is done to let participants know how they might feel so that when they do feel that way, they have anticipated the feeling and can continue to learn and not downshift.

✓ Orchestrating well-crafted questions ensures safety for participants and is a strong and useful skill for maintaining group rapport.

# 3 Read the Group

*It's not what you look at that matters, it's what you see.*

Henry David Thoreau

It has often been said that the whole is greater than the sum of its parts. This statement is never so true as when applied to groups. The key to reading groups is to learn to see the group as a whole, as opposed to seeing the group as a collection of individuals. When reading the group, the goal is to see the forest of trees and the patterns that exist, not just the individual trees. It is reported that some 30 million bits of incoming data bombard the human nervous system every minute. Many argue that the bulk of that data is not important. The gifted presenter knows not to get mired in the details when reading the group and instead to recognize patterns and pattern disruptions.

To help you get a handle on how to read a group, this chapter explores the essential ability from several perspectives. First we discuss recognizing the type of group based on two characteristics—high internal familiarity (the participants know each other) and low internal familiarity (the participants do not know each other)—and knowing the choreography for each type. This is followed by a discussion of participant types, how to identify them, and the ways to connect with each. Next comes the choreography that initiates and maintains group formation with a positive group dynamic. The chapter concludes with strategies to recognize and support group learning, processing, and development.

## RECOGNIZING THE INTERNALLY FAMILIAR GROUP

### Case Study 1: They're Armed!

Have you ever presented to a group in which every individual is armed? As a nonsworn civilian, presenting to a group in law enforcement is an amazing experience because they are often armed while in the training room. This unique experience presented itself ten years into my (Kendall's) career, and the learning curve was precipitous. You may be wondering how a story about presenting to a group of police officers is useful to you, knowing that you may never do so yourself. True, you may never find yourself presenting to a group in law enforcement; however, you may find yourself presenting to groups that have extremely high internal familiarity, camaraderie, professional identity, and discipline. The patterns of group dynamics and communication found in groups with these qualities are universal across cultures. By deconstructing a case study using law enforcement, group dynamics will become clearer and you will discover the eloquent moves that can quickly form a group and prime the pump for learning. Because these human communication patterns are universal and cross-cultural, the choreography revealed in this case study can be applied to multiple contexts.

If there was ever a time when I needed to be perceived as credible in front of a group, it was presenting to a group of sworn officers as a nonsworn civilian. This story illustrates the importance of establishing credibility upon entering a room. The description that follows isolates and describes ways of forming a group while building rapport. These two processes intermingle and, as in this case, occur simultaneously.

On many levels, law enforcement is unique, but it also shares many of the same characteristics of other groups with high internal familiarity and professional identity. Its unique elements include a deep commitment to obedience and compliance originating from the rigor of a paramilitary model while steeped in esprit de corps. As an example, when a presenter says "Good morning" to a group of officers, they quickly respond back with "Good morning." This is contrary to, say, a group of high school teachers. When a presenter says "Good morning" to an audience of high school teachers, getting half the group to respond is considered doing well.

Opening with "Good morning" when you do not know the group and they do not know you can put the audience in emotional retreat because credibility, rapport, and relationship have not yet been established. We suggest that the first word to permeate the ether in the room be a specially delivered statement designed to establish credibility and, in the case of this highly formed law enforcement group, to intrigue. Intrigue is achieved by making a statement about the participants that they do not think you know about them. It is the upper right-hand pane of the Johari Window (see Figure 3.1). The point of the opening statement is to tell them you know something about them that they know but they did not know you knew.

**Figure 3.1**    The Johari Window

| | |
|---|---|
| Participant knows something about self that presenter also knows | Participant knows something about self but doesn't realize presenter also knows this about the participant |
| Participant knows something about self but presenter doesn't know | Neither participant nor presenter know |

*Source:* Adapted from Luft and Ingham, 1955.

Here is the opening statement I delivered at the two-day training on facilitation skills for police and sheriffs who facilitate a leadership institute for law enforcement: "Facilitation is like policing. The trained eye sees what the untrained eye misses. Artful facilitation, like policing, relies on the deliberate, conscious, and strategic deployment of skills toward a desired outcome. Over the next two days, the hope is that you will see what you have always looked at in ways you never did before."

As the delivery of the opening statement began, I was standing still, breathing low and relaxed—it was a credible stance. My voice was narrow in modulation. Pauses were silent and still. I made eye contact with participants. This pattern helped establish credibility. Also during the delivery of this statement, the group shifted in unison from a rigid posture to a more fluid posture. Together, they entered into the moment and began to be a group beyond just law enforcement; they were beginning to be a group of learners.

Nonverbally, what happened? The goal, as with any opening, was to get the group to do something in unison. It can be anything, as long as it is in unison. It might be to laugh, to breathe, to nod, or even to subtly shift their body posture. The opening statement contained several catalysts directed at achieving the goal of creating response in unison. First, "Facilitating is like policing" was intended to link my expertise to their expertise. The expected and realized nonverbal response was stillness. "The trained eye sees what the untrained eye misses" and "deliberate, conscious, and strategic deployment of skills" were two phrases that zeroed in on the skills police know they have. By uttering these two phrases, I revealed that I knew something about them, which they did not know I knew. The choreography had been planned with the expectation to observe a recognizable shift in their posture. That meant a tilt of the head, a shift of the bodies, and breathing deeply. All three responses happened in unison.

Finally, the phrase "the hope is that you will see what you have always looked at in ways you never did before" was delivered with the idea that they would settle into their seats. The settling was recognized by an increase in the fluidity of their breathing and a reduction in the tension of their muscles as seen in their faces and in the lowering of their shoulders. In the 30 seconds it took to deliver the opening statement, credibility was established, rapport was building, and the group was forming.

The choreography was subtle, eloquent, and deliberate. Take a look at the text in Figure 3.2. The choreography, e.g., pauses and gestures, is described in the bracketed inserts.

**Figure 3.2**   Opening Statement With Choreography

[Credible voice] "Facilitation is like policing." [Pause] [Right hand lifts as elbow moves to 90 degrees] "The trained eye sees" [Pause with a frozen gesture] "what the untrained eye misses." [Pause] [Whisper voice] "Artful facilitation," [Pause] "like policing," [Pause] "relies on the deliberate," [Pause and beat gesture; increase volume with each stated attribute] "conscious," [Pause and beat gesture] "and strategic deployment" [Beat gesture] "of skills toward a desired outcome." [Pause; drop gestures to your side] "Over the next two days," [Pause with a frozen gesture] "the hope is that you will see" [Pause with a frozen gesture] "what you have always looked at" [Pause with a frozen gesture] "in ways you never did before."

## Case Study 2: The Texas Line Dance

———————————————— ❖ ————————————————

As a member of the National Academy of Science and Mathematics Education Leadership, I (Kendall) have made several visits to the University of Texas, Austin, over the years to work with the Dana Center staff. Austin is famous for its music, and every visit guarantees good music, good food, and good dancing. Dancing in Texas often includes the line dance, and when done well, from an anthropological perspective, the line dance is a delightful example of an ad hoc group that forms quickly. At the beginning of the dance, whether they know the steps or not, people get up and take a position on the dance floor. As the music begins, those who know the steps start right in. Those in doubt look to others for clues and leadership. Eventually and quickly, the steps are learned and the synchronized dance takes form, with dancers moving in unison to the beat of the music.

At the Dana Center training, a group of about 40 leaders in mathematics and science education met for two days of training that focused on forging partnerships and strengthening collaborative groups. When participants entered the training room, the internal familiarity was high; they scanned to see who was in the room to find a familiar face and eventually found a place to sit. As participants milled about and sipped their coffee, they caught up on family stories, talked about local happenings, and discussed details related to work. As the start time approached, they began to take their seats, often still engaged in paired conversations. Although participants knew each other and their movements were fluid, they were not yet a formed group, fully present in the room. Each individual conversation was unique and anchored in a past moment. As an internally familiar group, the opening impact statement and choreography were designed to first acknowledge the group, then honor their progress on the project, and finally focus them in the moment on the content at hand.

The opening statement went like this: "As we know, groups exist on a continuum from novice to expert. Where a group exists on the continuum is independent of the length of time the group has been together and is dependent on the group's level of craftsmanship, efficacy, interdependence, and flexibility. When individuals link together, they become something different. Relationships change us, reveal us, evoke more from us. Sometimes it is only when we join with others that our gifts become visible, even to ourselves. As you think about the achievements you each bring from the groups you represent, how might you move your groups from wherever they are on the continuum to even higher levels of expertise? Our time together is about moving along that continuum."

———————————————— ❖ ————————————————

Similar to the opening statement from the police training, this statement was delivered with a deliberate and strategic choreography, one sprinkled with variations in voice range, powerful pauses, both credible and approachable gestures, subtle changes in location, and a whispered voice of passion supported with syncopated beat gestures. And like the group of police officers, this group of educators shifted from stillness to fluidity, represented by a gentle rolling of movements across the room like the calm swells moving across a peaceful ocean—moving in real time with a pattern of unison.

As an effective presenter, you want to know where a group sits along the novice-to-expert continuum of group development, and there are several ways of doing this. Grinder (2008) suggests that you initially pay attention to where participants look as they take their seats. If they are generally looking at the presenter's location, even when the presenter is not there, they are a group, although they are a group that does not yet have the emotional safety necessary to establish a positive learning environment. With that data, as an effective presenter, you may modify the opening statement or the first 5 or 10 minutes of the presentation to acknowledge resistance, a current group experience, a shared group emotion, or a group energy source.

If there are a few quiet conversations among pairs in the audience, they are not a wholly formed group, yet they are comfortable enough to engage with whoever is sitting next to them. In a sense, they are exhibiting a sufficient level of emotional safety within their small groups. By recognizing these two easily observable details, you can determine where the group is in its development and open your session with two or three strategic moves that focus attention in the moment and create synchronicity of participant response.

One of our favorite and very effective strategies that we use to initiate group development is "Like Me." It is eloquently simple yet can be implemented along its continuum from transparent to invisible. Transparency is present when the presenter introduces the strategy by explaining what it is, why it is being used, and how to do it. For example, the presenter might say, "We are going to use a strategy called 'Like Me' to find out who is in the room and to surface what some of the commonalities might be among those in the room." These commonalities include role, expertise, experience, and familiarity with content matter. The presenter would continue, "How it works is that one of us will make a statement. If the statement is like you, stand and say, 'Like Me!' As you stand, look around the room to see who in the room is like you." Statements used during this activity might include the following:

- I am an elementary school teacher.
- I am a middle school teacher.

- I am a secondary teacher.
- I am a school site administrator.
- I have been teaching for over 20 years.

When participants acknowledge statements that reveal multiple connections among the group, group formation is accelerated and strengthened. Many in the group doing the same thing, in the same way, at the same time also accelerates group formation.

An intentionally nontransparent example of this group formation activity comes from a session we delivered to academic faculty at a large West Coast Class A research institute. Knowing that professors of physics, chemistry, linguistics, and other academic disciplines from a famous research institute may not feel particularly comfortable standing and saying with exuberance, "Like Me!" we anticipated more participation with a subtle synchronicity. In fact, it is unlikely that you will experience that sort of behavior from a group of doctors, lawyers, CEOs, or CFOs. To get these folks to scream "Like Me!" the gifted presenter must recognize what "screaming" looks and sounds like in these groups. In the case of the academicians, the situation was set up like this: "Now that we have a map of our day, let's get a sense of who is in the room, the disciplines represented, and your collective experience so we can frame the day to be most effective for you. Raise your hand when these statements apply to you." About 80 faculty attended this session, and for this group, screaming "Like Me!" was represented by tentative, halfway raised hands, subtle hand lifts off the arms of the chairs, and a few nods.

What is important to recognize is that every response, like every nonverbal pattern utilized by the presenter, has characteristics of range, intensity, and frequency. In the case of the professors, the range was narrow—held close to their personal space—although they eventually were in unison when they responded. Not the first or second time; developing this group took a little longer. In fact, they did not really loosen up for about 30 minutes, but by the end of the invisibly implemented "Like Me," their tentative and inhibited responses were in a state of unison; the group was well on its way to being receptive to the messages and open to considering the ideas presented.

A fascinating collateral result of this activity is the emergence of unstated group norms. These norms are unstated because they are the presenter's behaviors mirrored by the group. They are tacit norms in that they are implied, not explicitly taught. Specifically, as the presenter, you would raise your hand in a manner that models full participation while simultaneously saying, "Raise your hand . . ." modeling the desired and appropriate group behavior. Participants unconsciously comply and thus develop the norms of listening and responding to you. This activity also models the norms of participation and full inclusion.

You may be wondering what the "Like Me" statements sound like and how they might be constructed to identify important elements that support group formation. They might relate to the professions present and the experience in the room (e.g., "I am an elementary teacher," "I have been teaching for over 20 years"). It is also effective to insert some humor in the statements; this introduces the unstated norm that it is okay to laugh in this training. Claudette intersperses humor throughout her presentations, often beginning with statements such as "I consider chocolate a food group," and "I exercise every day," followed by "I exercise regularly," and then "I think about exercising." Laughter is guaranteed at this point, and laughter contributes to a powerful emotional state that supports and accelerates group formation and individual learning.

So far we have identified ways of recognizing where a group exists along the continuum of group formation, specifically looking at groups with high internal familiarity. We have also explored how opening statements establish credibility and can accelerate group formation. Next, we explore how to recognize and form groups who have little or no internal familiarity, as is often the case with audiences at regional and national conferences.

## RECOGNIZING THE INTERNALLY UNFAMILIAR GROUP

### Case Study 3: The Short Course

When presenting to a group that has little or no internal familiarity, you must quickly establish group safety, which is akin to one-on-one rapport; the intention is to open the lines of communication such that emotional threat is low and receptivity of the message about to be delivered is high. As an effective presenter, of course you establish credibility and build group formation, but the individual participant's emotional safety comes first.

Many of us have delivered short courses at regional and national association conferences. Typically, these run anywhere from a half-day, to a full-day, to a multiday session. Participants generally have little internal familiarity and little in common. Commonalities that do exist might include association membership, profession, role, or identity. By knowing even this much, you can use the information to choreograph a powerful opening that accelerates group formation and sets the stage for a productive session while creating a safe environment.

At one of these short courses, participants arriving alone often enter the room silently and generally find their seats in a direct fashion. Few initiate a side conversation with a stranger. While sitting, they may scan the conference program or take a few quick glances around the room. Mostly they sit facing in the direction of the presenter's location, even if it is empty. Movement tends to be less fluid; participants are generally more still when compared to how they might move when engaged in a conversation with a person seated next to them.

As an effective presenter, knowing your audience and reading the patterns are important to choreographing an opening. In the case of this short course with low internal familiarity, it is useful to include patterns of credibility and an opening statement that moves the group to a synchronicity of behavior in your opening dance. Sound familiar? It should; the pattern is the same for any group. It is both the content and the context that are unique for each audience. Since you cannot possibly know the context that will resonate with each participant, we suggest that you use a model of audience types to connect with individuals in the group. By understanding a generalized participant type model, you can be more effective at setting contexts that will resonate across diverse and unfamiliar groups.

As professionals, we wear many hats. And by that we mean that we inhabit many identities or roles. For instance, when Kendall was director of a university center of education, his hats included faculty, peer, director, colleague, subject matter expert, supervisor, subordinate, manager, and project director. We also have many identities outside of our professional lives. These might include wife, mother, aunt, daughter, sister, niece, grandmother, daughter-in-law, and oldest child. At a family reunion, you might well have all these identities at the same time, depending on who else is there. What a challenge!

In your professional life, your identities carry with them certain expectations from others. And your behaviors are unique for each identity. For instance, your identity in a meeting might include colleague, peer, subordinate, or superior, and these often determine how, when, and if you participate. When attending a professional development session, your level of interest, perception of relevance, and responsibility may also influence how you frame and participate in the experience. Likewise, participants' intentions will drive their attention. By surfacing, framing, and addressing their intentions, you can more effectively deliver content and design the processes that support participant learning.

There are many models that you can use as scaffolds when reading a group. The model we find most useful was first introduced by Silver, Strong, and Petini (2008) and suggests four types of audience members:

scientists (what are the patterns), professors (tell me more), inventors (what can I create with this information), and friends (more time together). As with any model, we respect this one for its usefulness while understanding and acknowledging its limitations.

In the case of this model, the expressed caution is to recognize that no single person is limited to a single identity. Everyone transitions from one identify to another depending on many factors, including context and history. The purpose for using this model is to ensure that opening statements have something for each of the four identities. Like the VAK model described in Chapter 2, Silver, Strong, and Petini's (2008) model is useful. And we suggest that by having knowledge of and expertise in both, you will be able to use each model as a lens to make sense of incoming data. Whichever lens makes the most sense and is most useful in helping you better understand the incoming data, that is the one that is best to use in that moment.

Table 3.1 lists the four audience types and examples of presentation strategies. Referring to this table when designing your presentations will ensure multiple connections for each audience type.

**Table 3.1** Four Audience Types Based on Silver, Strong, and Petini

| Audience Type | Considerations When Presenting |
| --- | --- |
| Scientists | They want to know why the content is important. They are often intellectually satisfied with the addition of graphs and data, and they appreciate having structure in the presentation. |
| Professors | They want to know what is important and how to remember the content or apply the skills taught. They often respond well to citations, feedback, and practice. |
| Inventors | They want to know what to do next with the information. They are creative and like to explore new ideas, discover new patterns, and express their new learning. |
| Friends | They want involvement and engagement with others in the room. They often respond well to stories, emotional hooks, and group activities. |

The strength of Silver, Strong, and Petini's model comes in recognizing the variety of participants in predictable categories. Knowing that all four types will be in your audience forces you to design a presentation that incorporates and balances cooperation, collaboration, academic references, data, and exploration. There is no formula suggesting that 25% of the time be spent on each audience type. It is up to you to determine what will be the most effective balance among the four types. By appropriately reading the group, you can determine when they are more or less engaged and modify your delivery accordingly to increase engagement. For instance, if you notice a decrease in engagement during an activity, you may introduce some data in a graph or provide a relevant quote or citation. If you notice an increase in attention and engagement, then you have discovered that the group is more scientist and professor, so you can continue in that frame as long as it is effective and you are achieving your goals for the session.

## MAINTAINING GROUP FORMATION

Think of a session that you attended, and recall how you left the room. Did you leave alone? Did you walk away with someone you did not know at the beginning of the session but had developed a connection by the end of it? Either way, it may have been an effective presentation in that you learned something. The second situation, however, exhibits evidence that the session created a new connection and most likely resulted in deeper learning. And that deeper learning came from the relationships created and choreographed by the presenter—a presenter who not only created a strong group, but also sustained that sense of a learning community throughout the session.

As mentioned earlier, the brain is our social organ and learning is a social act. A five-day institute that we conducted on instructor development provided a fertile foundation on which to build and maintain strong group formation. Participants attending this session had low internal familiarity, were often scientist and inventor types, and at the beginning of the session were low on the friend identity. Interestingly, by the end of the five days, friendship was everywhere.

If we recall that what we are looking for when reading a group is unison of behaviors, then recognizing when the group is out of sync is as helpful as recognizing when it is in sync. When a group is out of sync, it is often a good indicator that group formation has waned. When it does this, your goal is to bring synchronicity back to the unison of response. Many nonverbal strategies can be used in the context of reestablishing group synchronicity, including the following:

1. *Show, Don't Say:* This delightful strategy simply requires that you insert a pronoun in place of a noun that is visually displayed on an easel or PowerPoint slide. For instance, your slide may have several instructions

and information about an activity, including the page number corresponding to the participant's packet. By saying "Turn to *this* page" and using a frozen gesture directed at the actual page number, you force the group to look at the screen in order to gain access to the missing information. When a group is not in sync, this strategy can reestablish synchronicity, as evidenced by everyone looking to the screen at the same time.

2. *Yellow Light:* This strategy can be used in a multitude of contexts, from creating and maintaining emotional safety to foreshadowing difficult content to informing participants that they are going to do something and thus priming the pump to gain unison of response. A yellow light is a warning statement placed in the middle of a content paragraph (e.g., "As we finish this deep dive into dialogue, we *will then have our midmorning break.* Dialogue is grounded in . . ."). Often when a phrase anchored in physiological needs has been inserted, the group responds with a collective shift, nod, or acknowledgment. Smoothly and invisibly, you reestablish group formation, as evidenced by the synchronized response from participants.

3. *Pause:* The ubiquitous and ever-applicable pause surfaces again. The intent here is to get a group to do something (e.g., look at the presenter) at the same time. Imagine that you are presenting and you realize the group is in sync. You may notice some folks shifting in their seats, some shuffling papers, others texting, some even side-talking. To increase the probability of having everyone in the group look at you in unison, thus reestablishing the group, pause and look intelligent. You can even change location if you want. This amazingly simple skill takes time to master, and we remind you that if you want to look intelligent during a pause, keep your mouth closed and don't stare at any one person in the group. The silent yet sustained pause (about three seconds) accompanied with a look that resembles thinking can work wonders at getting the group to look at you.

## SMALL GROUP TO LARGE GROUP

Often in learning environments, to accelerate learning and deepen understanding, presenters organize adults into smaller learning groups. Dividing the whole group into smaller working groups has positive effects and influences, including the creating and maintaining of a more emotionally safe learning environment. One challenge facing presenters when doing this is to recognize the groups that are on task and those that are off task.

As a presenter, from the whole group frame, you can attune yourself to the attention level, recognize rapport, and assess levels of interest. From the small-group activity level, you can do the following:

- recognize whether the groups are on or off task
- recognize whether they are engaged or not
- determine the level of rapport within each small group
- assess how much learning is taking place
- recognize the degree of group development

To read groups within groups, the process is the same as reading one person. The difference is that when watching a small group, you look for when its baseline patterns deviate from the larger group's baseline. When members of a small group go off the baseline of the larger group, for instance, their voice volume goes higher than that of the collective group, but this does not mean they are off task. What it means is simply that their voice volume got louder. As a presenter, notice the shift and wait a few seconds to hear if the small group returns to the large group's baseline volume. If it does, no intervention is necessary. If it does not, then it might be time to stroll over and assess the situation. Since direct management of a group of adults is often not a good idea, the intervention might just entail listening and inserting a thought or suggestion during one of their pauses. Interestingly, as with elementary schoolchildren, proximity has influence with groups of adults. Instead of getting the group back on track, it may run the risk of downshifting the group by appearing like direct management. To stay effectively dissociated from the situation, presume a positive intention and reframe the conversation; on-task behavior often follows.

For example, on one occasion we were working on inquiry lessons with a group of high school science teachers. The group worked hard throughout the morning. During a midafternoon small-group activity, one group began laughing and their voice volume became louder than that of the collective group. As one of us approached the group, one teacher looked up and simply said, "Hey, we are off task and we will get back into it. We just needed a little mental break." Left alone again, within 30 seconds they were back on task, as evidenced by the decrease in their volume, each participant leaning forward toward the center of the group, and a renewed focus on the work on their table. We never had to utter a word; all it took was to slowly approach the table while looking at their work. They managed themselves with a gentle nonverbal nudge on our part. Rapport was never broken, and learning continued.

Rapport in small groups is recognized the same way as it is between two people. Is there fluidity and mirroring? If yes, the group is in rapport. If not, decide whether you want to approach the group to gather more data. For instance, in the previous example, the evidence that the group was off task and not in rapport was voice volume. A presenter may approach a group that appears out of rapport because they seem to be off task. The presenter may have just misread the group, or the group may actually be out of rapport because they are finished or don't know what to do next. In both cases, the data is very useful for the presenter, who can use it to choreograph the next move or transition phase.

## READING THE GROUP FOR LEARNING

Determining how much learning and group development are occurring is a bit trickier than just looking to see if a group is on or off task. When someone learns something, there are no direct nonverbal signals that say, "I know this, and this is how I know it." So as an effective presenter, you must gather more data. One way to determine whether they are learning is to watch the group behaviors. If each group is within the baseline of the whole group, then it is generally safe to assume they are engaged with the content. Roaming the room and listening to snippets from each table's conversation is a good strategy for collecting data. Generally, when groups are leaning forward during an activity and using credible voice patterns, they are probably on task and learning. So effectively monitoring small groups is enhanced by your ability to recognize subtle shifts off their credible-approachable baseline voice patterns. From our experience, the group that is off task first in an internally familiar group is often the one highest in the organization's hierarchy. They mentally left the workshop and are in new virtual reality. Like the holodeck on the USS Enterprise, they are back on campus, at least virtually.

To formatively assess whether learning is taking place, you can ask content-specific questions, ask for a demonstration, create a flipchart presentation, or engage in a number of other on-demand tasks. The important point here is that you can truly only read the group from the perspective of whether they are on or off task and whether they are in or out of rapport. In most cases, groups that are on task and in rapport are engaged with the content and learning.

## GROUP ATTRIBUTES

When adults gather to participate in a training or workshop, whether for a single day or multiple days, the group will develop a personality over the duration of the training. Classroom teachers know this because each semester and school year bring a new class of students, and with them a new group personality. At the secondary level, with five to six periods a day, each class section has a unique personality. The personality develops over time, and on bad days it may morph into something unrecognizable and savagely challenging. In some cases, teachers look forward to specific periods with positive anticipation while anticipating others with less enthusiasm. Given the gamut of group personalities, how wonderful would it be if we could implement specific strategies that actually influence a group's personality? Is it possible?

We know from experience that a group attending a session, no matter its length, will develop a collective personality. When the session is over, the group will have a collective identity and personality different from the sum of the individual personalities of each participant. The group will form unique connections based on the common experience they had at the workshop. As an effective presenter, your choice lies along two paths. Do you let the group form themselves and accept it as is? Or do you influence group development to create the memory, connection, perception, and identity that you desire? Certainly, the second path is preferable; otherwise this chapter would be over at this point.

As you may already recognize from the previous chapters, inserting attributes you would like to see in a group begins with your opening statement. In the case of the law enforcement session, my (Kendall's) intention was to have the group personality be intrigued, humorous, academic, and thoughtful. Each of these attributes was alluded to in the opening statement, and I verbally and nonverbally modeled each attribute.

In the following example, history preassigned the attribute of boring to the audience. The challenge for the two instructors was to shift that group's attribute to interesting.

## I REMEMBER YOU—YOU TAUGHT THAT REALLY BORING CLASS

Have you ever had to present a topic that you thought was boring? Well, if you thought it was boring, then most likely participants thought it was too. As presenters, many of us have found ourselves in a situation where the content is somewhat less compelling than we would like. For instance, some organizations have annually required workshops on topics such as CPR training, hazardous materials, emergency procedures, and educational law. Certainly, CPR is not boring, but what may result in people thinking it will be boring is having the expectation that attending the session will be like last time and nothing new will be learned. What is fascinating about this concept is that it is the anticipation of boredom that sets the expectation and frame that participants will be bored. If a participant walks into the room expecting to be bored, and the presenter does not reframe that anticipation, the participant will most likely be bored. Our attention is focused by our intention.

## AN IMPRESSIVE IMPRESSION

As participants, police officers have a delightfully gifted ability: to look interested when bored out of their minds. They also have honor and the attitude to be respectful. So when they attend a session that has a reputation of being boring, they appear attentive and, because of honor and esprit de corps, will sit though just about anything. Participation at this level of engagement is like driving the Loneliest Road in America while on cruise control set at 25 miles per hour—you'll get there, but the trip can be numbing.

Working with police officers, I (Kendall) encountered a pair who taught a class that by all accounts had the reputation of being boring. So boring, as the one officer told me, that given the choice between sitting through the session and having a root canal, most officers would pick the latter. Now that is boring!

These two instructors attended a five-day course on instructor development, which was anchored in adult learning theory and constructivist learning. During a group activity, I wandered around the room, monitoring group engagement, when the two instructors stopped us and said, "This adult learning theory and group work is fine for some groups, but we teach a class that is really boring and no one wants to be there. The class is required, and they have to attend. We just don't think this stuff will make a difference in our class."

As a presenter, I lit up with excitement thinking that a fantastic opportunity had just surfaced—a chance to reframe their learning from "this won't work" to "this will work." The conversation continued.

I asked, "Do you ever see any of your participants months or years later?"

They said, "Yes, because we are all officers and work together in the same agency, we run into each other quite often."

I continued by asking, "When you run into the participants sometime after the class, what do you think they are thinking when they remember that you were the instructors?"

Laughing, they responded, "They probably think, oh my gosh, I remember you. You were the instructor of that terribly boring class I took. Oh well, it wasn't your fault it was boring; the class was mandated."

So I commented that perhaps having the reputation of a boring instructor for a boring class is a reputation they would rather not be associated with. I then asked, "What if you could reframe that perception and expectation? What if, by using the skills from this session, you could shift participants' perceptions in such a way that the most boring topic becomes interesting?" They immediately became intrigued, and I told them that the next segment might have some useful strategies to help reframe their reputation from boring to engaging and useful.

The next training segment dealt with lesson design. I proceeded to incorporate nonverbal skills and some lesson design elements that ensured high engagement and learning. The short answer to the "boring" officers' dilemma was that their opening statement needed to name boredom as a culprit and reframe the content from a compelling perspective that participating officers could not ignore. In their case, the new opening statement mentioned that in 90% of cases when officers used CPR, it was used on a family member. So they went on to ask, "What might surface for you today that will make a difference for your family tomorrow?" Not only did the opening statement have a huge impact on participants' attention, the lessons they developed gained such a reputation that when they talked with participants months after the training, the participants often commented on the cool activities they had done in their class. (We will return to this story in the chapter on task, process, and group development to illustrate in detail the successes that these instructors had.)

I know that these instructors had success because they attended our advanced instructor development session some months later and reported on their success. They told us that they used the skills they learned from our session. Evidence of their success emerged during their sessions when several participants shared their opinions. They said that when they were driving to the session in the morning they were not looking forward to the class and just wanted to get through the day. They told the instructors that they never thought this class could be interesting. They concluded by saying how surprised they were at how fast the time passed, how much information they found useful, and how much they enjoyed the instructors.

❖

This story has a lot to do with reading the group because the instructors learned how to recognize when participants were and were not engaged, attentive, and learning. By reading the group and incorporating solid adult learning theory structures, these two instructors went from boring to competent and engaging in one class period. They incorporated an opening statement that named the resistance and reframed it into a statement steeped in values and honor. They also incorporated tasks and processes that supported learning through active engagement instead of through lecture and PowerPoint.

## KNOWING WHAT TO PAY ATTENTION TO

The ability to accurately read a group is essential to effective presenting because it is the data source from which you make decisions throughout the day. Like any good presenter, we all have our outline, plan, and outcomes for our session. We must plan. And we all that know when the session begins, following the plan requires adjustments in real time. Sometimes the adjustment is to completely throw out the plan and dance in the moment. When making adjustments, we need to know whether they were effective. The key is to develop the perceptual acuity to see what we need to see in order to respond in the most effective ways.

There is an adage that only half of what we see is important and knowing which half to look at is the mark of a genius. We are not here to claim genius by knowing which half. Rather, we hope to catalyze your senses to see what they have always looked at in ways that they never have. In the workshop setting, each person reacts uniquely. For presenters, various questions emerge: What do I pay attention to? How do I know that what I noticed is important and accurate? How do I know what to pay attention to and what to ignore?

Kendall used to bodysurf as a young boy in Newport Beach, California, and there is an important lesson to be learned from this. When you spend any time at the beach, you come to recognize that waves come in sets. As you watch the sets roll toward shore, you watch for the one wave that stands out, the one wave that is off the baseline of the group of waves. Once you see that wave, it is the wave you want to ride. The same holds true when watching groups.

Groups have movements that are recognizable as waves; think of them as ripples of energy. There are waves of interest, waves of laughter, waves of attention, waves of boredom. And they often emanate from specific locations. Identifying the person who is the point of origin for a wave is one useful key to reading the whole group because this person often influences the group. If you notice the origin as it is happening, you can encourage the wave or dissipate its energy. In either case, you are being proactive about group dynamics and the result will be a more productive session.

You may be wondering, what is a point of origin? Think about a time when you presented at or attended a session and you noticed that when something humorous was shared, one person would always begin to laugh before anyone else, and anytime that person did laugh the group would start to laugh right away. That one person can be thought of as the laughter pebble. Like a pebble dropped in a pond, the ripples emanate from that point of origin and spread across the entire surface of the pond. That person's laughter was the pebble, and the waves of laughter rippled through the group.

In every group, there are pebbles that serve as the catalyst for laughter, intrigue, and break time. There are also pebbles representing the "I'm bored" or "break time" seat wiggle. Learning to watch for the waves and identifying the pebbles of origin constitute the art of reading a group. By reading these signs, you can anticipate what the group needs and can be proactive. For instance, let's say you have identified the "break time" pebble. You notice the pebble shift, so you immediately insert a yellow light by saying, "After we finish discussing this important point, we will take a short break as we transition to our next topic that many of you may find intriguing." The group takes a wonderfully calm breath, exhales slowly, and increases its attention for the remaining moments. The potentially distracting energy is dissipated. By proactively recognizing for the need for a break before the participants themselves perceive this need, you take care of them. The key here is that the break may not necessarily have been planned at this time, but the "break time" pebble shifted, and recognizing that shift, you knew you needed to do something to prevent the wave from reaching the group. If the wave reaches the group, the probability increases that folks will begin to pay less attention. By catching the wave before it hits, attention is maintained.

When you know what to pay attention to and look for the pebbles, you start to refine your ability to spot them. Identifying patterns is a natural skill that we all have. The brain, in all its wonder, is amazingly adept at recognizing patterns. It is excellent at recognizing when something does not belong or is different. Throughout human history, this acuity was essential to survival. Today, the ability remains even though predators no longer roam and threaten in our urban and suburban enclaves. One of our most acute senses that help us recognize when something is not part of a pattern is our sight. We can detect even the slightest motion of an object relative to its surroundings. Recognizing the pebbles is about noticing that slightest of motions.

To begin to develop and heighten your perceptual acuity of group dynamics by recognizing various patterns, try the following activity, which I first encountered in a session on advanced group dynamics by Michael Grinder.

## Practice 3.1 | Developing Visual and Auditory Acuity

The purpose of this exercise is to enhance your visual and auditory acuity related to recognizing pebbles and waves in groups. To make this as effective as possible, it is best if you are not presenting but rather sitting off to the side with a broad side view of the audience. An excellent opportunity to do this is when copresenting. At one point when your partner is presenting, take 10 minutes to do the following:

### Visual Acuity Development

1. Put on earphones and listen to some loud, energetic music for 10 minutes (this reduces auditory input from the group and allows for a visual focus).

2. Find a location on the wall across the room just above the heads of the participants. This does not have to be a location that enables you to see the presenter. Stare at that point for 5 minutes.

3. After 5 minutes, find a location on the wall across the room that lets you see the presenter and a portion of the group. Stare at that point for 5 minutes.

4. After Steps 2 and 3 are complete, write down everything you noticed. Be data specific without judging or assigning causal relationships. For instance, do not write, "When the presenter made a joke, they laughed." This is not data; it is an inference. A sample data statement about the same occurrence might be, "The instructor talked, gestured to the group, stopped talking. The group immediately laughed."

**Auditory Acuity Development**

1. Put on a pair of eye covers like the kind airlines give you so you can sleep on the plane. This will eliminate visual input.

2. Wear them for 10 minutes while listening to the presenter and the group.

3. After 10 minutes, take them off and write down everything you noticed. Again, be data specific without making any causal associations.

As a result of this exercise, you will notice what you would not have noticed otherwise. For instance, when wearing the eye covers your auditory acuity becomes so refined that you can literally hear people shift in their seats, thumb through pages, side talk, and even breathe. Developing visual and auditory acuity is the foundation to effectively reading a group.

## SUMMARY

✓ There are two types of groups: high internal familiarity (the participants know each other) and low internal familiarity (the participants do not know each other).

✓ If the participants are generally looking at the presenter's location, even when the presenter is not there, they are a group, although they do not yet have the emotional safety necessary to establish a positive learning environment.

✓ By making statements that reveal multiple connections between participants, the presenter accelerates and strengthens group formation.

✓ Group safety is akin to one-on-one rapport; the intention is to open the lines of communication such that emotional threat is low and receptivity to the message about to be delivered is high.

✓ Strategies that can be used to reestablish synchronicity include Show, Don't Say; Yellow Light; and Pause.

✓ Rapport in small groups is recognized the same way as it is between two people.

✓ Generally, when groups are leaning forward during an activity and using credible voice patterns, they are probably on task and learning.

# 4 Balance Task, Process, and Group Development

*The greater the loyalty of a group toward the group, the greater is the motivation among the members to achieve the goals of the group, and the greater the probability that the group will achieve its goals.*

Rensis Likert

How do you know when it is just right? You know, that perfect blend of content chunking with engaging activities that together form a strong group steeped in personal learning. Might there be ways to evaluate and select the appropriate activity and execute the right dance to reach the desired learning outcome? This may sound like a question fresh out of a course on curriculum design, and it is, with subtle variations. When thinking about effective presenting, it is also important to consider the delicate balance between selecting the most effective processes to be used to support the tasks to be completed while monitoring group development. Task is the *what*. For instance, the task might be to offer an effective paraphrase. Process is the *how*. Building on the aforementioned task, the process might be something like this:

> Working in pairs, Person A explains the strategy. At the presenter's signal, Person A stops talking and Person B offers a paraphrase.

Group development is a dynamic state that involves the interplay of socially and intellectually collaborative relationships among group members. Social collaboration includes resolving conflicts, working together on tasks, celebrating achievements, participating fully, listening and acknowledging, and valuing diversity of ideas. Intellectual collaboration includes thinking constructively, making decisions, solving problems, reflecting on experience, withholding judgment, examining assumptions, and suspending biases. Balanced presentations artfully craft processes that engage the learner, develop the group, and bring every participant into the learning experience.

We believe that one of our main objectives as presenters is to have all participants leave the professional learning opportunity with enhanced skills and knowledge as well as the desire to apply the learning in their work environment. We can positively influence that outcome by balancing task, process, and group development. Whether this particular group of participants is together for a day or a year, their learning can be enhanced by paying close attention to the relationships within the group, the tasks they are asked to perform, and the protocols they are asked to follow in order to complete the course work.

## THE PERFECT BALANCE

Imagine being at a training session as a neutral observer, akin to being the fly on the wall, invisible to the group yet present. You notice a healthy-sounding hum in a room packed with 120 participants attending a multi-day training on effective presentation skills. The presenter displays new information on the screen and the front easel. Taped on the wall is easel paper with neatly written information in alternating colors. Near the front end of the side wall is the agenda, clearly printed and posted, and next to it is a list of 15 strategies and enough blank space to add several more. The back wall has information about university credit, housekeeping details, and other topics that are management related and content related. On a side wall, numerous easel papers display participants' work; as the days progress, that wall space fills with more of their work. By the end of the session, participants own the room and their learning.

You notice from your balcony view, the position that allows you to see the group dynamics, that participants change learning partners throughout the week. During some activities, participants get up and move about the room such that no part of the room remains unoccupied or unexplored. You also notice a delightful dance step linked to energy. As the cycle of participant energy waxes and wanes, a pattern of presenter moves emerges. When a waning phase seems eminent, the presenter consistently and effectively shifts the participant energy to higher levels. This shift is eloquently and strategically deployed based on the energy level of a few specific individuals so that the energy of the whole group never drops to significantly lower levels. Only the energy of a couple of participants begins to drop, and the presenter uses those few waning participants as barometers to gauge the direction in which the group is heading. By reading the barometers,[4] the presenter effectively and proactively adjusts to avert the impending lulls in energy and attention from the entire group. The group energy remains constructive and positive.

Another pattern that emerges is the deliberate syncopation between loosely and tightly structured protocols. You notice that the first few protocols that require participants to engage with one another are loosely structured; there are few instructions, and the boundaries defining how participants interact and how they will talk are more general than specific. The loose protocols allow participants to enter the territory safely, free from risk; find their place in the room; make connections with others; and find out who they are in relationship to others in the room. These loose protocols are intended to establish participant rapport and initiate healthy participant trust, efficacy, and interdependence. Determining when to use tight or loose protocols depends on the context and the degree of group development.

About an hour into the session, the first tightly structured protocol appears. It is used for a content-rich segment that makes participants accountable to each other. Since the seeds of rapport and trust were planted and tended to in the first few minutes, the intellectual and self-reflective conversations emerging from the tightly structured protocol are rich; they begin to catalyze participants' learning and accelerate the connections between what participants are learning and how they will apply it in the work they do. Protocols are the linchpin that makes for a good presentation, which frees the presenter from having to rely on charisma. This is important because charisma is not always deliberately replicable or reliable, and it focuses energy on the presenter and not where it should be focused: on the participants.

## WHY PROCESS AND GROUP DEVELOPMENT?

The power of process emanates from the quality of the choreographed protocols, and the most effective protocols have multiple benefits:

- balanced participation
- increased engagement
- accelerated learning for each participant
- individual and group accountability
- positive interdependence among participants

Together, these benefits contribute to maintaining a safe learning environment. If you want groups to get better over time, it would be best to include structures within the protocols that support reflection time for participants to construct and share how they feel about how they have been working together. By becoming more aware of how they are learning, and interacting as a group, they are more likely to move to higher levels of expertise and proficiency.

Without well-structured and appropriate protocols, participation is unbalanced, learning does not occur for every participant, and there is little accountability, A session with poor task, process, and group development sets the stage for several possible derailings, including a takeover by the raving extrovert; a grotto of solitude and hiding for the introvert; a never-ending traffic jam for the detail-oriented Type A participant who cannot see the map or anticipate what lies ahead; a field of daydreaming for the kinesthetic participant, where being off task is not noticed; and a straightjacket that impedes participation and blurs the focus of learning for adults with attention deficit disorder tendencies.

Reflection is a process skill that encourages strong group development. It allows groups to identify where they are in the stages of group development. Protocols create space for everyone in the group to participate and contribute verbally, emotionally, and intellectually. Protocols also allow for the insertion of norms, and when participants follow a protocol they are honoring the norms. By choosing the right protocol, such as the Paraphrase Passport (see Figure 4.1), the presenter ensures that every person is listened to and is acknowledged.

A final consideration for considering group development concerns how groups make decisions. Are participants making decisions together or as individuals? Effective, well-constructed protocols support group development in the arena of decision making. Protocols designed to provide space for every participant to contribute ideas, to advocate, and to inquire are protocols that support effective decision making.

---

**Figure 4.1**   Paraphrase Passport

*Information Processing: Exploring and Discovering*

**Process**

- Provide a prompt for conversation.
- Groups explore a topic:
  - Person A makes an initiating statement.
  - The group pauses for 5 seconds.
  - The next group member (anyone) paraphrases the previous statment before inquiring or adding related ideas.

- Repeat the pattern as time permits.
- To close the talk, the group constructs a summarizing and organizing paraphrase of the full conversation.

**Alternatives**

- The person designated to paraphrase could be sitting next to Person A, and other participants round-robin from there.
- After a speaker has been paraphrased, any member may inquire or add ideas.

*Source:* Garmston and Wellman, 2009.

## PROTOCOL STRUCTURES

Protocols define the behavioral and intellectual boundaries for an activity. How much leeway participants have within the boundaries ranges from broad to narrow. A protocol that allows a lot of leeway—freedom to move about intellectually and behaviorally—is considered a loose protocol. One that narrowly guides intellectual thinking and behavioral interactions is considered a tight protocol. Table 4.1 illustrates one of each. The loose protocol is open and ambiguous in its definition of what participants will discuss and how they will interact. The tight protocol clearly defines and guides the conversation by identifying who will talk, when, and how.

| **Table 4.1** Loose and Tight Protocols | |
|---|---|
| **Loose** | **Tight** |
| Stated verbally with no visual exit directions: "Turn to your neighbor, and share an important point from the morning session. You have two minutes." | Visual exit directions followed by process as given/process as understood<br><br>In pairs (count off "A" and "B"):<br>• partners silently read the first paragraph<br>• A paraphrases the first paragraph<br>• B provides an example (no cross talk)<br>• partners silently read the second paragraph<br>• B paraphrases the second paragraph<br>• A provides an example (no cross talk)<br>• continue through all eight paragraphs, rotating roles. |

In Table 4.1, the loose protocol is given verbally with no visual exit directions. It may have been previously planned and scheduled in the presentation, or it may be inserted in the moment because the group needs to do some processing or move around to infuse energy into the room. In either case, it is casual, brief, and somewhat ambiguous. The tight protocol is visually displayed and clearly part of the original presentation plan. It is precise and well defined, and it sets clear parameters.

You may be wondering how one decides what protocol to use, loose or tight. There are many criteria from which to select, and there is no hard-and-fast rule identifying which to use. We have found three criteria that seem to consistently guide our thinking when planning: (1) the nature of the task, (2) where the group is in their group development, and (3) the group's disposition toward the content. By disposition, we mean the level of resistance to the content, the psychological safety, or the emotional attachment to the outcome (see Table 4.2).

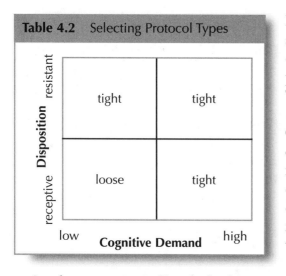

Table 4.2    Selecting Protocol Types

As you deliver a tight protocol, look at and point to the PowerPoint slide (or other display) when delivering each step of the protocol's visual exit directions. This move is called *third point* (Grinder, 1997). As you recall from Chapter 2, third-point communication is directed to an object in the room. By using this method to deliver the protocol, you make the display the manager and you are free to roam the room and engage with participants as needed.

Third point has a deceptively simple appearance. Simply looking at a screen image or easel pad when delivering a message, as opposed to looking at the group, is a challenging skill for many presenters to learn because it requires deliberately breaking eye contact with the group. In the United States, people tend to equate direct eye contact with rapport, empathy, and trust. We suggest that eye contact should be maintained when engaging in content and learning and severed when managing or directing the group. One substantially negative effect of looking at the group when delivering a tight protocol is the perception that the presenter is overly managing the group. This perception is compounded when a presenter says, "I want you to read the first paragraph." When a presenter uses *I* to direct participants to do something, the implied relationship between presenter and adult participant is one of power. Using *I* does not contribute to interdependence, individual accountability, or learning. When the participant is not compliant with a verbal request that includes an *I* statement, it introduces the possibility that the noncompliance is due to a relationship issue.

Third point actually preserves rapport when used to deliver exit directions. Some alternatives to *I* when delivering exit directions for a protocol include *the, our,* and *your.* For instance, "The first step is to read the paragraph. Your next step is for person A to. . . ." An even better way to deliver exit directions is to use a Benefit, What, Why, How frame. Notice the absence of any *I* statements here:

"You will come to understand how others view the 7 Essential Abilities by following the Paraphrase Passport protocol. It will ensure that each of you understands what the other is thinking and provide you the opportunity to practice your paraphrases. In pairs . . . [go to PowerPoint slide]."

Utilizing this frame and shifting language from *I* to *the/your* is congruent with adult learning theory. Together, these moves support interdependence as well as personal and group accountability, and they accelerate learning because the shift in language is more respectful and nonthreatening.

The tight protocol can be followed up with a process as given/process as understood (PAG/PAU) move (Garmston & Wellman, 2009). When using PAG/PAU, after giving the protocol instructions, you can say to the group, "Raise your hand if you are an A. Someone please tell the group what A will do first." After hearing the response, ask, "And what will B do?" It works well to have the group answer in unison. If it is a multistep protocol, the progression is recorded on the slide or chart paper. By looking at this display and pointing to each instruction as you go through the PAG/PAU, you are teaching the group to defer to the instructions and not to you for direction. This frees you from having to manage their behavior. Continue to ask questions until you are comfortable that the group understands the process (e.g., "What questions do you have about this activity before you begin?"). This prevents confusion and wasted time as the participants can then focus on the task at hand, and not the protocols. Then release the group to begin the activity.

When releasing the group, you may notice that not every participant immediately gets on task. To increase the degree of compliance in a respectful manner, it is very effective to stand still for about 20 seconds while the group begins the task. By standing still, breathing low, and not engaging in direct eye contact with participants, you are letting them know that you trust them to get to the task. If some participants do not immediately start, you can nonverbally redirect them to the work, which is often all that is needed for them to begin the task. Our experience is that even the most resistant participant quickly complies and begins the activity when the presenter stands still for that powerful and influential 20 seconds.

## TASK AND THE BLOOMIN' PYRAMID

What do you want participants to know and be able to do? What level of understanding do you want them to attain? Setting specific outcomes related to knowledge, skills, and abilities is important in any presentation or training. It is also critical to decide what level of understanding is most appropriate for each outcome. To achieve this goal, we rely on Benjamin Bloom's (1956) taxonomy, a classic model for identifying cognitive levels of understanding (see Figure 4.2).

By identifying the level of understanding that you want participants to master, you can better choose the process that best supports that outcome. Generally, as you progress higher on Bloom's taxonomy, the more structured the process and the more time required to spend mastering that task and/or cognitive ability. To ensure that activities align with the desired levels of understanding, we have found the Understanding by Design model (Wiggins & McTighe, 1998) to be very useful when designing curriculum. Levels of understanding in this model include the following: explain, interpret, apply, have perspective, empathize, and have self-knowledge. Self-knowledge is important from two perspectives: self-awareness (What am I learning?) and group development (What is the

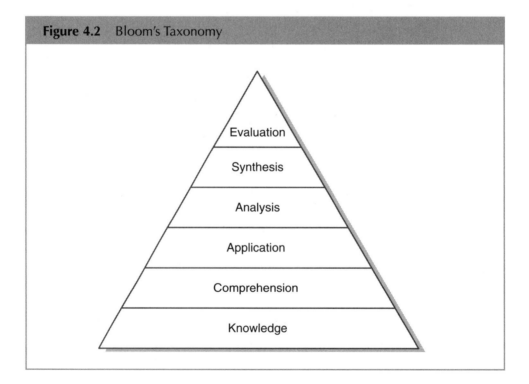

**Figure 4.2**    Bloom's Taxonomy

group learning about itself?). Effective presenters monitor individual and group learning by gathering and displaying data such as participant work and using reflective protocols that require small groups to verbally share their learning with the whole group.

## BALANCING BASED ON PARTICIPANTS' FRAME OF REFERENCE

The participants' frame of reference is an important criterion to consider when selecting the process to support the learning task. There are many combinations and possibilities: the willing participant, the captive participant, the welcome program, the contentious program, the one with low emotional connection, and the one with high emotional connection (see Figure 4.3).

If participants are resistant to the topic or display a contentious attitude, protocols that are tightly structured will focus their learning on the content while reducing emotionally negative tensions to lower levels that are more conducive to learning. Protocols that do not maintain appropriate emotional tension run the risk of allowing this tension to elevate to where it manifests itself as aggressive resistance, conflict, or engaged neutrality. The rule of thumb that we follow is this: the more

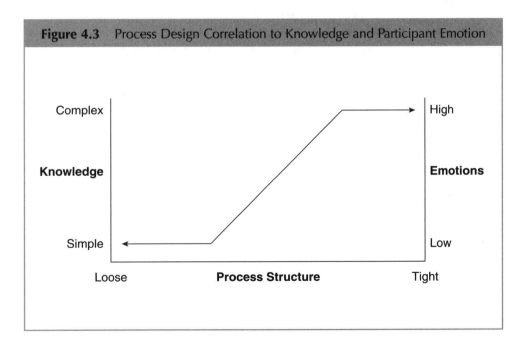

**Figure 4.3**  Process Design Correlation to Knowledge and Participant Emotion

contentious the issue, the tighter the protocol used. If participants don't trust each other to take care of each other, then they have to be able to trust the process if they are to get any work done.

By knowing your group ahead of time, you can design a training that balances their needs with the desired outcomes and that will accommodate their emotional frame.

## LISTENING, AND ACKNOWLEDGING WHAT IS NOT SAID

### A DRESS REHEARSAL

It was our second day of a five-day institute on building collaborative groups, and we were an hour into the morning segment on strategies and structures to support dialogue. Over 100 superintendents, principals, and central office curriculum leaders were in attendance. The content was complex and the activities intense. To encourage an emotionally safe learning environment, we had small groups work through an activity that modeled a dialogue by simulating a real conversation relevant to their work in schools. As they engaged in the activity, each individual personally selected one or two specific strategies to practice. They were encouraged to select strategies that would stretch their learning. The last step in the small-group protocol was for participants to reflect on their learning and to share how their newly acquired skills affected their participation and influence on others.

The success of this collaborative group activity was dependent on the structure of the initial question guiding their dialogue breakout session. The positive presupposition was that the participants were indeed learning. By design, the conversations they had in their small groups were about their own personal learning. When giving exit instructions for the group reflection activity, we foreshadowed the next activity by saying, "Be prepared to share your learning with the whole group." When foreshadowing what was to come next, we watched to see if the group remained fluid and calm in their breathing; we listened not to what they were saying, rather to what they were doing. Since they remained fluid and calm in their breathing, we knew they would share when the time came. Had this not been the case (e.g., if they froze and stopped breathing), we would have known they were not emotionally safe enough to share. As effective presenters, our options are proactively set in the carefully constructed instruction, "Be prepared to. . . ." This statement does not say you *will* share; it says you *may* share. This is more ambiguous and only alludes to the possibility of sharing. By using a phrase that leaves options open, when the time comes to end the activity, we can share or simply move on to the next topic based on where the group is in terms of their safety and development. If the group is safe, we share. If not, we can try to recover and insert humor or use some other tactic that gets the group to shift into a safe mode, or we can move on to the next topic.

Foreshadowing is supported by several strategies and moves, including Yellow Light (see Chapter 2) and exit directions. The yellow light is a useful metaphor signaling a transition or foreshadowing the next step in a training session. A well-placed yellow light provides participants with an array of useful data. By saying, "In your table groups, share what you are learning and be prepared to share your learning with the whole group," when you later deliver exit directions, participants know that not only will they be sharing with their small group, they will also have the opportunity to share with entire group. In a sense, the small-group reflection conversation serves as a rehearsal, or prelude, to performing in front of the whole group.

Another influence of Yellow Light in this example is the reduction or elimination of group silence. Have you ever been at a workshop where the presenter said, "Who would like to share?" and no one responded? As a participant, it is uncomfortable. As a presenter, the silence is downright deafening! At that moment, as a presenter you realize that safety is out the window, rapport is shot, and trust is waning. Inserting a yellow light decreases the likelihood of that awkward silence.

The following are five ways to insert a yellow light and monitor group safety to ensure that no deafening silence precedes group sharing:

1. *During exit directions, with the group breathing low:* You may remember that the most effective exit directions are delivered visually. In this example, the same is true for the yellow light. Using an easel or PowerPoint slide, list your exit directions for the activity. At the end of the protocol, using a different color, write "Be prepared to share your learning with the larger group." As you say each line of the exit directions, look from the screen to the group. When you say the last line, be sure you have peripheral vision to see if participants are breathing low. If they continue to breathe low, you are fine and the group is fine. In all likelihood, the sharing will go smoothly.

2. *During exit directions, with the group breathing high:* Follow the same protocol as in #1. This time, however, when you say the "sharing" statement,

you notice that the group shifts to breathing high. With that evidence, it is safe to conclude that participants are not feeling safe and sharing will not come easy. The most important thing here is your ability to recognize high breathing in a group. When you do, congratulations for your excellent perceptual abilities! To recover and get the group to a level of safety that increases the odds that someone will share, go to #4.

3. *During exit directions, when you anticipate that the group will breathe high:* Follow the same steps as in #1. The difference here is that you will be proactive instead of finding yourself in a reactive state like in #2. If you anticipate that whole-group sharing will be met with resistance, then soften the exit direction by saying, "We may take some comments from tables after you share in your small groups." By using the word *may,* you are indicating a tentative option to the group. That way, if you decide that they are not feeling safe after table sharing, you can go on to the next activity without having to explain why you did not have the whole group share. Also, by saying "from tables," you are indicating that what might be shared will not be an individual's learning but rather the learning expressed at the table. This makes the sharing more anonymous, and anonymity increases safety. Another way to add anonymity and to make participants feel safer is to say, "At the end of the five minutes, your group will share some of the common experiences from the people at your table." You can then randomly choose the table's reporter before starting so that person can prepare by taking notes.

4. *While roaming the room after giving exit directions, when the group breathed high:* Assuming that #2 is a reality, what do you do to reestablish safety? One strategy is to roam the room and listen. As individuals share with their table groups, when you hear something of high interest from the table perspective, insert yourself into the group and ask, "Would someone mind sharing that insight with the whole group?" By getting a commitment from several tables ahead of making your request to the whole group, there is a good chance that silence will not permeate the room when you ask, "Who would like to share?" Or better yet, if you have a few commitments from your room roam, you might consider asking this delightfully ambiguous question: "Some rich conversations revealed some powerful insights. Who would like to share some thoughts that emerged from their group?" This ambiguous question allows for anonymity to be maintained by whoever responds. As an example, when someone does respond, the group does not know if this person's statement is about his own learning or someone else's. As a result, the person sharing is able to save face and not reveal what he does or do not know. Falling short of this does not mean failure. With some groups, it is part of the culture that personal learning is not

shared. And that's okay because sharing group learning is also effective in supporting individual learning. Although it is not their own learning that is publicly revealed, in essence, people are still thinking and learning.

5. *If you forgot to do it during exit directions:* This situation can occur in two ways. The first is that you had planned to tell the group to be prepared to share and you failed to mention it. The other is that you decide in the moment. For instance, as you roam the room listening to small-group conversations, you hear some rich ideas. You also feel that the whole group would gain knowledge and understanding if they could hear these ideas. So you decide to insert a yellow light. One way to do this is to write on the easel "Most important learning." Write this while the groups are still talking so that they do not notice you writing. Then, call them back as a whole group. Look at the easel and say, "We will continue the conversation around this prompt. What, at your table, has been the most important learning for you? Talk at your table for 90 more seconds, and decide what you would like to share with the group." This prompt remains ambiguous and, more important, adds an element of critical thinking because the question asks participants to evaluate quality. They have to decide what is most important. By asking the question this way, you anchor the conversation in content and add the element of value. People tend to pay more attention in conversations when levels of value are present.

Taking the idea of getting groups to share one step further, you can decrease the duration of a silence by adding structure (a protocol). If you want to ensure that all tables share, then add structure under the guise of humor. For example, you could say, "Thank you for coming back. We are now going to hear from each table some thoughts on their learning. To do this, we will begin at this table and track around the room this way. In order to know who will be doing the sharing, please scan your group and decide which person has the darkest hair. If more than one person in the group has the same color hair, then the one with that color whose hair is the longest will share." Now everyone at the table knows who will speak, and it is random—no one is singled out based on an idea. The strategy of selecting such an attribute to determine who shares often adds energy to the room. Other attributes that work include the person whose back is more parallel to one of the room's walls, the person who is closest to the exit, or the person with the most interesting shoes. You can also use this to help the group get to know each other more by focusing on such attributes as the person who lives the closest to where the session is being held, the person who stayed up the latest last night, or the person who regularly gets up the earliest. The possibilities are virtually endless.

Another yellow light is related to time. Group work is a ubiquitous and essential feature of adult learning situations. The challenge for presenters is getting a group's attention when they are engaged in conversation in a way that preserves rapport and honors their engagement. One strategy, first introduced by Grinder as a yellow light, we label the Last Call (see Figure 4.4).

You can use the Last Call when getting ready to bring a group back from small groups to whole group. The strategy is simple, the choreography nuanced. Timing for inserting the last call is determined by two factors: the group's collective volume and whether you sense that it is time to move on.

All groups cycle between high and low voice volumes, and the cycle generally lasts five to seven seconds. If you take the time to listen to the collective room volume when groups are engaged in activities, you will hear the volume increase and decrease. Sometimes it is very obvious, while at other times it can be very subtle. This is a normal pattern. One place where it can sometimes become embarrassingly obvious is at a dinner party. Have you ever attended a dinner party with lots of people milling about in the host's home? People were laughing, conversing, drinking, eating. You may have found yourself talking with someone, and in that conversation you missed something that the other person said because the group was too loud. So you ask her to repeat it. She begins to repeat it, loudly. Suddenly the group quiets, and that person is left finishing her sentence in a voice way too loud for the silence. The lone voice fills the room like the howling of a wolf. Luckily, if the group is friendly enough, laughing ensues because of the social faux pas. This is an example of a cycle that drops to silence.

For those of you who teach, you easily recognize when the collective volume of the class cycles up and down. And when the class volume gets too loud, you will manage and the class quiets. It is a natural cycle, and by recognizing that, you can use it to your advantage when managing or working with large groups. In the case of a yellow light for the Last Call, we suggest the following steps:

1. Take a position in the room near the location where you have been presenting content (Figure 4.4, location 2).

2. From that location, stand still, use indirect eye contact, and breathe low.

3. As you hear the group volume decrease, raise your hand in a relaxed manner, not stiff and erect.

4. Using a voice pace that is much slower than your usual teaching voice pace and a rhythm that is at the opposite end of the continuum from where the group is, say, "Thirty more seconds."

5. Continue to stand still, breathing low and maintaining indirect eye contact.

6. As the time elapsed approaches 30 seconds, listen again for the next decrease in volume.

7. As you hear the decrease in volume, step quickly into the teaching location (Figure 4.4, location 1), with erect posture, low breathing, and direct eye contact, and say, "Thank you [pause, gesture with palm down] and please [pause, gesture to self] look this way."

**Figure 4.4**  Last Call

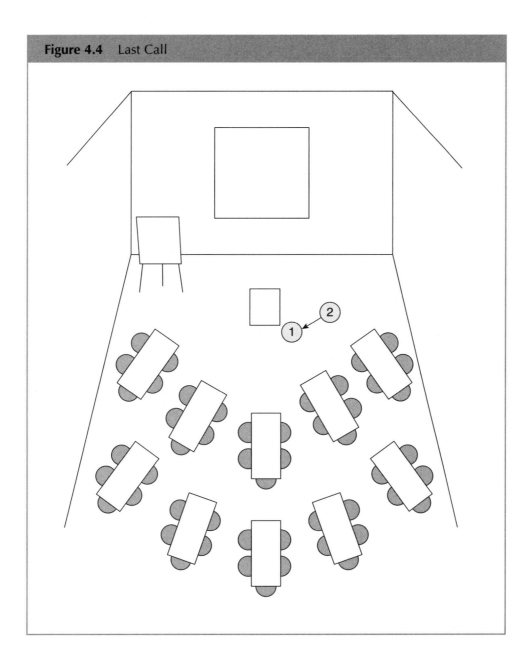

## WIGGINS ABOVE

This story is told with Grant Wiggins's support and approval as a way to illustrate how these skills can be quickly learned and effectively implemented with immediate success when groups are working and you want to get their attention. This skill is called ABOVE (pause) *whisper* (Grinder, 1997).

Several years ago, we brought Grant Wiggins to the university for a two-day intensive workshop on Understanding by Design, which was attended by over 90 middle and high school science and math teachers. Those of you who have attended Grant's workshops know the power of his interactive presentation style. And those of you with experience presenting also know the challenge of respectfully getting the attention of 90 energetic teachers who are deeply engaged in group work.

Grant knew my (Kendall) background in presentation skills, and in our conversations he showed an interest in learning different attention-getting strategies besides ringing chimes and dimming lights. We talked about ABOVE (pause) *whisper* and, with some casual training and coaching during the actual training day, Grant was ready to give it a try.

It was after lunch, and the group was actively engaged in a small-group task. All of the participants were talking, working, and learning. Grant was ready to get their attention. As he was nearing the time when he wanted them to reconvene as a whole group, he stood about three feet from the projector and, using a flat, monotone voice, he delivered a yellow light by saying, very slowly, "Thirty more seconds." With no eye contact with any participants, he patiently stood still, and as he heard the collective volume of the group decrease, he stepped toward the projector and uttered a word slightly louder than the loudest voice in the room. He paused and stood very still next to the projector while utilizing a soft yet prominent frozen gesture and then whispered a simple statement: "Our next step is to. . . ." Within seconds, the group was silent and attentive. The session continued right in step, as planned, to the next activity.

Grant successfully used this skill several times throughout the day. At dinner after the training, we reflected on the day. He was excited about the newly acquired skill and was amazed at the influence the skill had on the group. After the training, we stayed in contact for a few months and Grant reported back his successes using the new skill in his other training events.

The good news in this story is that the skills are learnable and with perseverance can be readily implemented with success. Of course, the skills do not work all the time; however, with a fully loaded tool belt of strategies, it is comforting to know that ABOVE (pause) *whisper* is a useful addition to any presenter's arsenal.

By inserting a last call with the collective volume decreasing, you build on the decreasing momentum of the group. They are already moving to a lower energy state; you are simply facilitating the process by contributing to the decreasing energy.

The opposite is true if you implement a last call while the group volume is increasing. That is like adding fuel to the fire. If you say "Thirty more seconds" while the group volume is increasing, two things usually happen. One is that the group does not hear you and you end up repeating yourself (one powerful indicator of when a management technique is ineffective). The other is that the group continues to get louder. In both cases, you end up shifting from proactive to reactive. Being reactive takes more energy and, when managing, results in fewer choices. And remember, anytime you revert to direct management of adult groups, you run the risk of being shot down.

| Practice 4.1 | Influencing and Monitoring Group Volume |
|---|---|

Many groups have enjoyed this exercise, but none as much as the police group described in Chapter 3. When working with law enforcement, this activity is often the most energizing and entertaining. This is an exercise you can practice while presenting and no one will know you are practicing.

1. Get the large group to work in small groups of four to eight. As they work, stand off to the side of the room and listen. Recognize the increases and decreases in volume. You will hear them. Listen long enough to identify the timing of the increase to decrease pattern.

2. Wander over to a small group, and engage in conversation with them. As you talk with them, simultaneously listen to the collective volume in the room. You are now going to do two things: first increase the volume of the whole group and then decrease the volume of the whole group.

   • To increase the volume, as the collective group volume increases, increase your volume as you talk to the small group. Continue to raise your volume in distinct, incremental steps. However, do not raise your voice volume like the clarinet increases pitch at the opening of Gershwin's "Rhapsody in Blue"; that continuous increase will not be as effective as distinct step increases. When it is done well, you will notice an increase in volume higher than the highest volume from the last cycle.

   • To decrease the volume, as the group volume begins to decrease, say a word or two to the small group at a volume slightly louder that the group volume at that instant. Then pause for a brief second and continue talking to the small group in an even quieter voice volume, again doing so in a stepwise fashion. Done well, this technique can actually get a group of adults to stop talking without any perceptions of direct management.

By offering structure through task and process, you can balance participation, increase engagement, and accelerate the learning of each participant. Structures often increase the probability of participant involvement. One of the reasons is that they can hold a spot for each person to contribute. Another is that, depending on the protocol chosen, participant accountability can be built in; by providing a protocol with accountability, you can increase the probability of participants fully engaging in the work. The following is an example of a statement that builds accountability: "During the next five minutes, please create a list of ways you might use this concept in your classrooms. When we reconvene as a large group, each pair will contribute three of their strongest ideas for application." Using this protocol and others can often increase the input of introverts and temper that of extroverts.

An appropriate structure offers direction and creates an environment safe enough for risk taking. Certain protocols lend themselves better to accomplishing particular tasks. Without protocols for large and small groups, as well as partner interactions, learning is often left to chance. We believe that teaching is a deliberate act and learning is a social activity. The conscious and deliberate use of structures that support task, process, and group development are essential if your desire is to bring congruence to teaching and learning.

## SUMMARY

✓ If you want groups to get better over time, you must include structures within the protocols that support reflection time for participants to construct and share how they feel about how they have been working together.
✓ Reflection is a process skill that encourages strong group development.
✓ Protocols define the behavioral and intellectual boundaries of an activity.
✓ Eye contact should be maintained when engaging in content and learning, and severed when managing or directing the group.
✓ Effective presenters monitor individual and group learning by gathering and posting data such as participant work and using reflective protocols that require small groups to verbally share their learning with the whole group.
✓ Protocols that are tightly structured will focus participants' learning on the content while reducing emotionally negative tensions to lower levels that are more conducive to learning.

# 5 Listen to and Acknowledge Participants

*Listening is such a simple act. It requires us to be present, and that takes practice, but we don't have to do anything else. We don't have to advise, or coach, or sound wise. We just have to be willing to sit there and listen.*

Margaret J. Wheatley

Two deeply human desires are to be listened to and acknowledged. How we listen and acknowledge contributes much to the quality of our relationships, and how we as presenters listen to and acknowledge participants contributes much to the quality of their learning.

As we think about participants in a learning environment, two tensions come to mind. First is their internal tension associated with not knowing or discovering that they don't know. The second is a self-inflicted tension created when, as the result of a well-crafted protocol, a participant publicly reveals to a group of colleagues in a professional setting what he

> Your role as presenter is to listen to and acknowledge participants as they learn by managing the balance between the cognitive tension of learning and the psychological tension of participating.

doesn't know. What is ironic here is that for learning to take place, tension must be present. The key is not to eliminate tension; rather, it is to manage the tension by reframing it from being associated with emotional threat to being associated with cognitive challenge. Not managing that tension can manifest itself in different ways, ranging from harmful levels of stress to behaviors of passive resistance. One situation in which psychological tension often arises is when participants are asked to practice a skill they have not yet perfected. Your role as presenter is to listen to and acknowledge them as they learn by managing the balance between the cognitive tension of learning and the psychological tension of participating. When well managed, the cognitive tension is high and the psychological tension is low. When poorly managed, tension is destructive because so much of the participant's energy is focused on reacting to a high emotional threat.

Siegel (2007) elegantly states in *The Mindful Brain* that "our brains are the social organ of the body" (p. 169). We know adults learn best when constructing their own understanding in an intellectually open and sharing environment that is personally relevant. Oliver Wendell Holmes is credited with saying, "Man's mind, once stretched by a new idea, never regains its original dimensions." It is this stretch that generates the inevitable and requisite cognitive tension that is essential to a powerful learning environment. The challenge for the effective presenter is knowing when and how to surface, nurture, and manage the tensions in order to maximize learning and group development.

In this chapter, we explore and examine recent findings in the field of neurology that support interpersonal intelligence. Second, to gain insight into the more effective practices while recognizing the less effective efforts, we present stories from the good and not-so-good memory vault of past presenters. Third, we look at the skills of listening and acknowledging from a group dynamic perspective, specifically identifying the significant participant behaviors that we want to surface. We close with a few exercises to support your learning.

## THE SAFE LEARNING ENVIRONMENT— A STATE OF RELAXED ALERTNESS

Our experience with adults in professional development settings runs the gamut from folks who participate fully to those who overtly resist activities and choose not to participate. The challenge for the presenter is knowing how to deliberately and strategically create an environment in which all participants intellectually and socially engages in their own learning. Listening and acknowledging help establish and maintain a state of relaxed alertness (Caine & Caine, 1994), a psychological state in which the emotional threat from revealing what you do not know is low and the cognitive challenge associated with learning new material is high. Because learning is a social event, the presenter must know how and when to create this powerful and artfully balanced learning environment.

The good news is that ensuring relaxed alertness and managing psychological tensions are possible and probable when thoughtfully choreographed. As you begin to understand more deeply the skills that support how to listen and acknowledge, your perspective about how you view tension may also shift. Tension, like conflict, is not a barrier that blocks learning and participation; rather, it is a fuel that propels learners as they navigate through fields of cognitive challenge and seize their own learning.

Tension is potential energy, the stored energy that when channeled effectively can be used to support learning. Without tension, there is no learning. Mortimer Adler, editor of the original series Great Books of the Western World, knew the importance of intellectual tension when he said, "The purpose of learning is growth, and our minds, unlike our bodies, can continue growing as long as we live." For Adler, this statement served as a mission that gave him life-long permission to acknowledge what he did not know and to reveal what he was learning. By holding his statement as a core assumption, we accept the challenge to create the pathways for adults to grow. We not only mean this metaphorically, we also mean it literally—in the sense of neurological pathways.

## THE NEURO CONNECTION

Neuroscience research conducted in the 1990s overturned an earlier deeply held assumption that brain plasticity decreased throughout an individual's lifetime and, at some point in midlife, ceased to exist. The good news is that we now know the brain is capable of modifying neurological pathways throughout our lives. This neuroplasticity allows the brain to "reshape and reorganize these networks, at least partly, in response to increased or decreased use of these pathways" (Willis, 2008, p. 426). Willis and fellow researchers have demonstrated that "after repeated practice, the connections [between neurons] grow stronger, that is, repeated stimulation makes each neuron more likely to trigger the next connected neuron" (p. 426). The tension between not knowing and knowing can be thought of as the energy source that fuels the physical reshaping and reorganizing of our brains.

What does this mean to presenters? Several things. First and foremost, all people can learn, no matter what their age. The key is to create an environment in which the brain is receptive to the messages presented. What researchers have discovered is that when adults experience cognitive dissonance, their receptivity to new ideas and new learning drops and the thinking part of their brain may even turn off all together. By effectively listening to and acknowledging participants, you can proactively short-circuit the downshifting cascade to maintain a receptive state of mind.

Like you surely have, we have seen many presenters who are effective at listening and acknowledging yet are unconscious of the specific nonverbal and linguistic patterns used. What that means is that when they are having a good day and have a malleable group, they are effective. But when they are having a bad day and the group is pushing back, they are not able to reproduce their effective strategies and moves. By relying on intuition to accomplish listening to and acknowledging participants, the unconscious presenter may lack a strategic advantage and may also experience her own downshift event when faced with a contentious group of resisters.

Bob Garmston, an outstanding presenter and mentor of ours, is especially gifted in this ability to listen and acknowledge. We deconstruct his choreography here to illustrate the dance of a presenter who is effective in this area. To the untrained eye, his dance appears effortless. His dance acknowledges the participant and, most important, involves and acknowledges the group. You may find it comforting to know that many presenters find this particular ability requires a lot of practice with many rehearsals in order to achieve a competent level of automaticity.

Learning new steps is a lot like breaking in new shoes: they pinch a little at first before starting to feel comfortable. Our suggestion is to give yourself some grace, be patient, and take it one step at a time. Although these moves are deceptively simple, they are not easy to master. It takes practice to reach the appearance of effortlessness. Once each skill is mastered, begin to combine them to master their dynamic interplay and influence. By being conscious and competent in this way, you will be able to replicate the dance at will.

## THE GOOD: LOW THREAT AND HIGH IMPACT

When presenting, every one of us has at some time asked the group a question. For some presenters, what follows is a long, sustained, and haunting silence. No one answers. Bob Garmston skillfully circumvents this silence, thus paving the way to socially engage the group in learning.

On the second day of a five-day institute, we were in a session filled with superintendents, principals, and central office staff. Clearly, these were knowledgeable and skilled experts, but they were initially reticent when it came to sharing ideas with the whole group, as evidenced by their tentative nature when first engaging in activities. This behavior is very common to newly formed groups. What we assert is that by choreographing specific moves at critical times, you can initiate and accelerate the development of a learning environment steeped in relaxed alertness.

For participants to perceive being listened to and genuinely acknowledged, Bob engages in the following choreographed dance. Standing in his expert location (Figure 5.1, location 1), he often closes with, "And this last point is perhaps the most important . . ." and he concludes the idea. He silently pauses and stands still while scanning the group with a relaxed breathing pattern. He takes a few steps to a new location where there is a stool or a tall chair (Figure 5.1, location 2). He sits, breathes deeply, and scans the group. This is the location where thinking and processing occur. Throughout the first day, Bob moved to this location when group processing, asking reflective questions, or taking audience comments. Using an approachable voice and stance, with his palms, up he asks, "What questions might you have? What thinking and musings are you having?" Hands immediately go up. We consistently see this group behavior when this presenter presents. It is as predictable as the sunrise. When he calls on a person, it is usually with a single word, "Please." As the participant speaks, the presenter sits still, breathes low, and maintains direct eye contact with the participant. Upon completion of the question or comment, the presenter's next words are often, "Thank you," followed by one of several paths: pausing, paraphrasing, or probing and inquiring.

❖

**Figure 5.1**  Choreography of Transitioning From Presenter to Processor

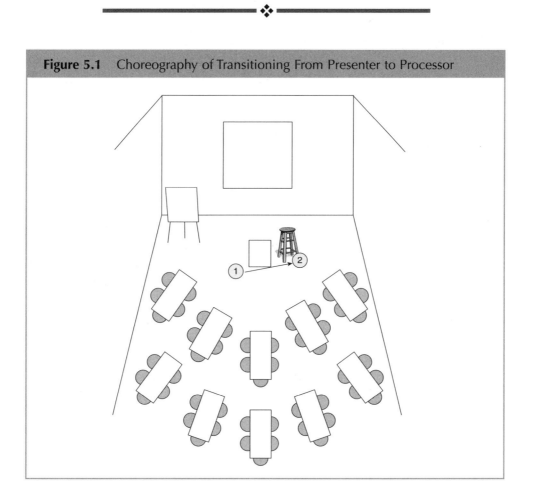

# PAUSING, PARAPHRASING, AND PROBING AND INQUIRING

Standing still, maintaining eye contact, and breathing low while a participant speaks is only the beginning of listening and acknowledging. The next steps include what you do following their contribution. Three fundamental skills are essential to demonstrating listening: pausing, paraphrasing, and probing and inquiring. Together, these skills contribute to participants' thinking and group development by causing them to engage in the experience of learning and extend their learning to personally and professionally practical applications.

## Pausing

We learned about how to effectively use the pause in earlier chapters. The same patterns of pause apply in this situation; however, the intention of the pause when we listen and acknowledge is to support participants' thinking and inclusion in the content. The effective pause is used when a participant completes the sharing of an idea. In the story we just shared, the presenter often and initially responds with "Thank you," using an approachable voice and a palm-up gesture, followed by a low-breathing three-second pause. Often the breath is visually overt, meaning that the presenter breathes deep enough so that participants can see his shoulders lift and chest expand. Participants often mirror the presenter's breathing pattern, and a mirrored breathing pattern is evidence of rapport. Their calming breath also supports their thinking.

## Paraphrasing

This skill requires eloquence and nuance. It is the paraphrase that ultimately provides participants with evidence that they were listened to. Once they know this, the paraphrase reinforces the acknowledgment.

An effective paraphrase it is one that reflects back to a participant the content of his comment with matching energy, linguistic modality, and emotional state. Such a well-delivered paraphrase is the apotheosis of rapport. The intention is to surface the participant's meaning in such a way that he recognizes the match between his own perceived meaning and the presenter's understanding. Paraphrasing is not about agreeing with the participant's idea, though; it is about understanding it. When the presenter establishes a clear and common understanding of the participant's comment, the group is free to consider the idea from a common understanding, which promotes thinking and participation.

The paraphrase is a sophisticated skill that requires the choreography of discrete syncopated steps within a fluid and dynamic environment. Because it is intended to reflect the content, energy, language, and emotion of the participant, it is best delivered using *you* language rather than *I* language. For instance, consider the following participant comment from a lesson study session using student work samples. Two paraphrases are suggested. The first paraphrase is delivered in a recommended format while the second paraphrase is delivered in a less recommended format. As you read the two paraphrases, think about how a participant might feel about being listened to and acknowledged.

> *Participant 1:* I really like that the parents don't doubt me in this matter.
>
> > *Paraphrase 1a (more effective):* Ah, you're appreciative of their support.
> >
> > *Paraphrase 1b (less effective):* So I am hearing you say that you like not being bothered by the parents.
>
> *Participant 2:* I love the program. But to implement it properly we would need more time, materials, training, and money.
>
> > *Paraphrase 2a (more effective)*: So for you it's about having enough resources.
> >
> > *Paraphrase 2b (less effective):* What I hear you say is that you need more time, materials, training, and money.
>
> *Participant 3:* This is the kind of program I can really get excited about—it challenges my students, respects their independence, and promotes collaboration.
>
> > *Paraphrase 3a (more effective):* So you really value self-reliance for your students.
> >
> > *Paraphrase 3b (less effective):* I think you are excited about this program because it challenges your students and respects their independence.

## Probing and Inquiring

After effectively using a paraphrase that clarifies the ideas being shared, probing and inquiring are two forms of questioning that can move participants' thinking to deeper levels. The probing question focuses and narrows, while the inquiry may broaden perspectives.

Using the paraphrase "So you really value self-reliance for your students," an example of a probing question or statement is "For you, what are some examples of self-reliant behavior?" And to ensure that this is a thought-provoking probe, an approachable voice and palm-up gesture are used to sustain rapport and support the continued flow of information among participants and presenter.

An example of an inquiry that may follow the paraphrase "I think you are excited about this program because it challenges your students and respects their independence" is "In addition to independence, what might be some other benefits to students using this program?" In this example, the inquiry suggests a cognitive lens that widens participants' perspective and opens their thinking to consider what they might not have considered before. Inquiring, when done well with appropriate nonverbal congruence, can seem liberating to participants because it surfaces options, as opposed to limiting or restricting them.

## FREEDOM FROM SELF

To be in a state of mind that is conducive to accessing the ability to fully listen and acknowledge, you must separate your self-identity from your presenter identify. Often without meaning to, we go autobiographical in our thinking. For instance, when listening to someone, you may think about a personal experience and listen from the framework of that experiential perspective.

> It is not about making a point; it is about extending participants' learning.

Sometimes you may listen from an inquisitive perspective to gain more information or detail for your own understanding. And sometimes you may listen to generate and provide solutions and move on to the next topic. In all three contexts, the listening was about your thoughts, not about the participant's contribution. To listen as a presenter, you should set-aside the "self" listening frames. As a presenter, when you listen to and acknowledge others, you support their thinking and promote their understanding of the material.

## THE LA DANCE—WHAT IT LOOKS AND SOUNDS LIKE

We have archives of video supporting the elusive Listen and Acknowledge (LA) Dance of freezing the body, breathing low, using direct eye contact, and maintaining an approachable stance. This may sound simple, but it is something we rarely see with consistency. The influence of the pattern is subtle and penetrating, as captured in the nuances of the dance. For instance, the specific volume and voice pitch of the presenter's "Thank you" is most effective when it matches the volume and tone of the participant who made the preceding comment. Also, the size of the palm-up gesture is important. Is it close to the presenter's torso, or is it extended in a way that the elbow is also extended beyond the torso? The appropriateness of the subtle nuances comes with experience. What is important is recognizing the range and intensity of each pattern and how those two qualities affect group dynamics.

The penetrating influence of the LA Dance results in the emergence of increasing participation to the extent that several participants add their comments and questions in a smooth and syncopated rhythm. Some comments are related; others are divergent. What is amazing is that there is a natural flow, the group is attentive, people are thinking, and the environment is in a state of relaxed alertness. The group dynamics are congruent with a positive learning environment, and individuals flourish in their own learning—there is, in the spirit of Csíkszentmihályi (2003), a state of flow.

We cannot overemphasize this important state of learning. We believe that every person perceives the world in her own way and that each individual makes meaning in her own way. In a group setting, a presenter cannot teach each person individually. So an effective presenter has to create an environment in which the group perceives a sufficient level of emotional safety to publicly engage in learning. The individuals who perceive personal safety while being part of the group can then begin to focus on their own learning. As they focus on their own learning, ideas are shared, the brain is engaged, and learning is socially constructed.

The quality and thoughtfulness of participant questions and comments are indicators of levels of rapport and learning. Hearing a participant say, "I am learning more about . . ." is a powerful indicator of learning. We have found that once one participant overtly reveals his learning to the group, others follow.

## THE BAD: HIGH THREAT AND LOW IMPACT

At a university in the western United States, I was a participant in a daylong workshop on workplace skills. The presenters were nationally recognized for the quality of their work and the applicability of their model in the workplace. After the initial opening, a hand went up in the audience. The comment was not solicited; rather, a participant happened to have something to say. As the hand went up, the presenter stopped midsentence and began walking toward the person whose hand was raised. About 10 feet from the participant, the presenter stopped, assumed a frontal position, and with a palm-up, straight-hand gesture that snapped into location (Figure 5.2, location 1), said in a credible voice, "Please." While the participant was making her comment, the presenter took a step closer to her and increased the intensity of the direct eye contact by breathing higher in the chest. When the participant finished her comment, the presenter said, "No . . ." and proceeded to give an explanation.

When the presenter finished, the participant said, "That is not what I meant. I am talking about. . . ." And this was said in a very credible voice, with sharp and pointed gestures. Two more rounds of this exchange continued. At the end of each round, the presenter took an additional step toward the participant (Figure 5.2, locations 2 and 3). By the end of the third round, the participant shifted her body from a credible seated stance to one where she leaned back, pursed her lips, and slowly looked around the room. She and the presenter had tried to dance, never got the steps in sequence, and eventually one of them decided to get off the dance floor.

**Figure 5.2**    Ineffectively Listening to and Acknowledging Participants

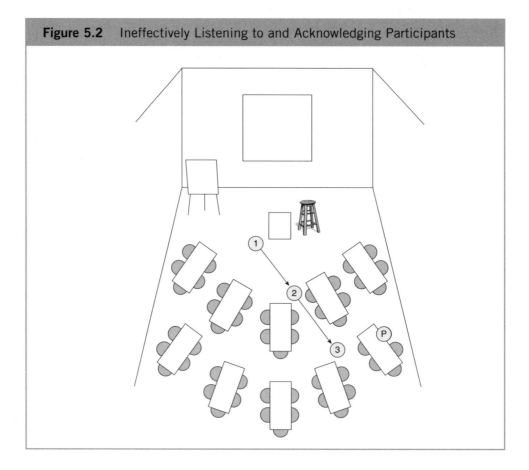

While the presenter and participant were trying to engage, the folks located behind the presenter initially turned slightly and silently toward one another. They never really looked at the other people at their table; rather, they kept their eyes on the presenter while their faces turned toward their neighbor. By the end of the three-step exchange, several pairs in the room began side-talking and paying little attention to the presenter or the participant who had asked the question.

Although the presenter later called for questions on four separate occasions, we noticed that 40 minutes passed before another participant posed a question or made a comment. Silence almost suffocated the room after the presenter asked for questions and then continued with, "Good, we will go on to the next topic?" This scenario was repeated four times during that 40 minutes. It was painful to watch because the group was no longer displaying behaviors associated with emotional safety and there was no evidence of individual learning since no ideas were shared or vocalized.

You may be wondering why this happened given that the presenter stood still and maintained direct eye contact. But she did not really remain still. She kept taking small steps toward the person making the comment. For some participants, these small steps can be perceived as "noise" because the movement interrupts their thinking. It is as if they are being verbally interrupted. The presenter also did not use an approachable voice, opting instead for one that was more toward the credible end of the continuum. Also, her gestures were not approachable. They were stiff and swiftly deployed, and the hand was held flat and straight as opposed to gently arched. In combination, these patterns can be perceived as a threat. So much so that the participant even apologized by saying, "I'm sorry, that is not what I meant." It was at that point that others in the audience began side-talking. The group judgment was such that the participant was not respectfully listened to or acknowledged. Emotional safety was low and threat was high. The room was tense.

Two presenters using the same fundamental patterns resulted in a slightly different choreography because of range and intensity, and the dances achieved very different outcomes. One was effective in surfacing ideas, opening lines of communication, and revealing evidence of learning. The other was ineffective. We tell these two stories in this chapter to illustrate the importance of being conscious of the skills related to range and intensity and understanding the nuances behind each skill.

## KNOWING ONLY ONE DANCE
## WHEN ANOTHER IS CALLED FOR

I observed a session where the instructor was a high kinesthetic, someone who exhibits several behaviors that can either enhance or interfere with learning. In this case, the pattern was disruptive. To think and to construct responses to participant questions, this presenter had to pace back and forth. It was not possible for him to stand still while listening. Another distracting listening pattern was also present: lack of direct eye contact. He could not maintain direct eye contact with a presenter for the duration of a question or comment. As a participant asked a question, the presenter would break eye contact and look toward the ground in front of him. About halfway through the question, he would begin pacing across the front of the room. He would also often interrupt the questioner and begin answering the question before the participant was finished, thus addressing a specific phrase, not the entire inquiry.

When the presenter displayed these patterns, the person asking the question often paid little attention to his response. While he was still responding, the participant would often turn to a neighbor and engage in a quiet side conversation or sometimes shuffle papers and scan the packet on the table. Some of the other participants turned and looked at each other, others stared off, some looked out the window, many shifted in their seats, others thumbed through the pages of their packets, and a few pulled out their BlackBerry and scanned their messages.

Watching this was enlightening because we should presume that the presenter genuinely wanted to answer the question to the participant's satisfaction. Yet the behavior that supported the presenter's thinking impeded the participant's thinking. It was disheartening to see a presenter oblivious to the negative influences of his own communication patterns on participants' learning, participation, and group dynamic. His communication patterns were established early on the first day of a five-day institute, and as the days progressed, fewer and fewer questions were asked of him. By the third day, he had morphed into a stand-and-deliver presenter with little if any participant interaction. Interestingly, and luckily for participants, this course was cofacilitated. The other presenter, a high visual who was skilled at the 7 Essential Abilities, had a much higher frequency of thoughtful questions than the other presenter. And when this high-visual person was presenting, participants paid more attention and were significantly more engaged.

The effective presenter does the following when listening and acknowledging participants: as a hand comes up in the audience (Figure 5.3, right-hand image), the presenter moves slowly away from the participant (from location 1 to location 2) to increase the distance from the questioner and to increase the peripheral vision in order to see the whole group. In contrast, in the left-hand image, notice the limited peripheral vision, which prevents the presenter from seeing three table groups, as indicated by the dotted lines. Compare this to the peripheral vision in the right-hand image, where by changing location the presenter can see every table group while maintaining attention to the participant who is speaking.

By moving away from the person asking the question, the presenter initiates four important influences. First, the person asking the question tends to speak louder the farther away the presenter is, allowing the group

**Figure 5.3**    Listening and Acknowledging Choreographed Ineffectively vs. Effectively

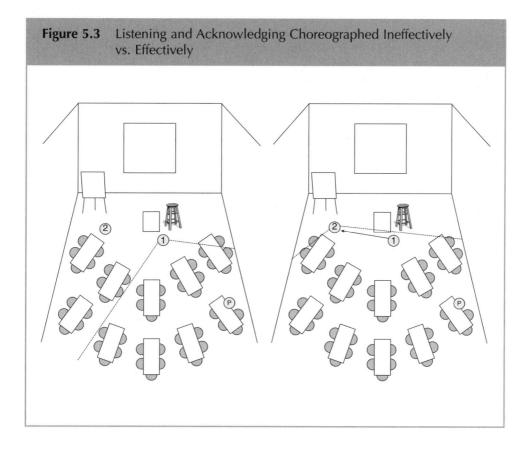

to hear the question without having to repeat it. Second, the group is physically included in the question because every group member is between the presenter and the questioner. Third, this new location helps keep the group engaged because they are all in the middle of the activity. And fourth, the presenter has shifted her peripheral vision so she can see the entire group and "listen" to the group's nonverbal reaction to the participant's question or comment. If the group perceives the question as appropriate, the presenter will know it is appropriate to answer. If the group perceives the question as not being appropriate, the presenter then has several options:

1. Ask the participant to explain his thinking in connection to the topic at hand.

2. Paraphrase or probe the question or comment.

3. Tell the participant that he can talk more about that interesting idea during the break.

Once on the other side of the room, the skilled presenter will stand still, establish direct eye contact with the participant, and call on him. She will listen, stand still, breathe low, and maintain direct eye contact with a slight head tilt and an invitational gesture until the question or comment is completed. Then, more often than not, the presenter will say, "Thank you."

Let's return for a moment to the story about the high-kinesthetic and high-visual copresenters. The high-visual presenter received more thoughtful questions, more follow-up questions, and more contextually relevant comments from participants that revealed their thinking and learning. Also, when this presenter listened to and acknowledged a person who was asking a question or making a comment, the other participants remained more still and generally maintained more direct eye contact toward the participant who was speaking. There was no side talk, and not one person pulled out a BlackBerry. It was astounding to see so much behavior consistent with being attentive.

So what patterns contributed to this group behavior? Those that support effectively listening to and acknowledging participants: standing still, using a frozen gesture, pausing, breathing low, changing location, saying "please" and "thank you," and paraphrasing. Two of these are explained in the following paragraphs, but it is important to recognize that although these patterns are explained discretely, in reality these skills are choreographed into a syncopated dance as fluid as water and as ubiquitous as the air we breathe.

## Standing Still

Standing still while listening supports psychological safety by sending the message to the person speaking that you are fully present and listening to what she is saying. How you stand is important. On one hand, you do not want to stand at attention like an officer in the Marines. It is not always bad to stand that way, but such a still and erect stance may not be conducive to supporting the flow of ideas. It generally is more effective to use a credible stance. Having your arms at your side with your hands open and relaxed sends a message of attention. Another element worth considering is a tilting of the head. People perceive a higher level of welcoming and friendliness when the head is tilted as opposed to being held erect over the shoulders.

## The Frozen Hand Gesture

The influence that standing still has on the perception of listening can be enhanced by using a frozen gesture. This type of gesture is an added accent telling a person that you are listening and paying attention. Using a frozen gesture is also a very useful skill that can support your own thinking and processing while listening. Done well, it can serve as the visual equivalent of direct eye contact. This is useful because if you think better when not looking at a participant, the gesture gives you permission to look away while paying attention, and then to process.

A first-year teacher provided this comment after attending one of our training sessions: "I noticed that I am able to recognize when students are actually talking about the math and when they are talking about other things. This was a learning experience for me. I was able to make more observations than I can remember, but from every observation I had something to learn."

## Practice 5.1 | Less Effective

This exercise is best done in pairs or small groups. One person is the presenter, and another person agrees to raise his hand and either ask a question or provide a comment.

Step 1: Presenter talks.

Step 2: Participant raises his hand.

Step 3: Presenter continues to talk and slowly moves away from the participant to a point where she can see, peripherally, the entire group.

Step 4: The presenter pauses and gestures to the participant to speak.

Step 5: The participant begins to ask the question or make the comment.

Step 6: The presenter immediately breaks eye contact, looks away, and steps to the side.

Reflection: What does the participant perceive? What did those remaining at the table notice?

## Practice 5.2 | More Effective

Repeat Steps 1–5 from Practice 5.1, replacing Step 6 as follows: The presenter maintains direct eye contact, breathes low and relaxed, and remains silent.

## SUMMARY

✓ How you listen and acknowledge contributes much to the quality of your relationships, and how you listen to and acknowledge participants contributes much to the quality of their learning.

✓ Standing still, maintaining eye contact, and breathing low while a participant speaks is only the beginning of listening and acknowledging. The next steps include what you do following their contribution. Three fundamental skills are essential to demonstrating listening: pausing, paraphrasing, and probing and inquiring.

✓ An effective presenter must create an environment in which the group perceives a sufficient level of emotional safety to publicly engage in learning.

✓ Standing still while listening supports psychological safety by sending the message to the person speaking that you are fully present and listening to what she is saying.

# 6 Respond Appropriately

*To listen closely and reply well is the highest perfection we are able to attain in the art of conversation.*

Francois de La Rochefoucauld

It has no doubt become clear that our idea of effective presenting is very much about behavioral skills and strategies. Many stories have been told about the presenter's behaviors as well as the importance of recognizing participant behaviors. This chapter is critical because it describes core communication skills that increase congruence between intention and perception. When communicating, there are two realities: the sender's intention and the listener's interpretation. We believe the meaning of communication is determined by the latter. The sender's intention is a hallucination because its meaning only exists in the mind of the presenter. Whereas reality, the meaning of the communication according to Grinder and Bandler (1975), is derived from the response received. When the listener's response aligns with the speaker's intention, we call that congruence.

In this chapter we offer stories from both ends of the continuum to include the inappropriate as well as appropriate responses. We explain how and why our responses are targeted to group dynamics and take a back seat to individual group members. We also explore how the skills supporting this ability enhance learning, maintain credibility and rapport, and may be used to reframe resistance.

## IT'S ABOUT THE GROUP

Presenters who respond appropriately maintain high credibility, rapport, and trust with their audience. They are responding to two audiences. The first and most important audience is the entire group. The second is the person asking a question or offering a comment. To preserve a group dynamic that supports a safe learning environment, attending to the audience is the most important responsibility, and as such the skills introduced in this chapter are intended to support the group.

Grinder has often said that the primary responsibility of a presenter is the safety of the group. How the presenter responds contributes to the level of safety in a group. By safety, we mean having participants in a state open to receiving and considering the message. Groups that perceive a high (emotional) threat are less receptive to receiving a message than groups that perceive low or no threat. Our intention when responding appropriately is to create an environment in which the group is receptive to hearing and considering the response, sometimes at the expense of the individual. You may find this idea intriguing, specifically that the presenter's intention to satisfy the audience may not satisfy the person who verbally contributed by asking a question, providing a comment, or answering a question. This concept is addressed in the Chapter 7 discussion of the Satisfy-Satisfy-Delay technique.

## THE SENDING-RECEIVING MISMATCH

Our first story about responding appropriately focuses on a presenter who believed that he was responding appropriately to the individual yet was unable to satisfy the group. The result was that the group shifted to high alert, unable to consider the message being delivered. The presenter was working with police officers who were also instructors in police academies, teaching young people how to be police. The academy programs are rich in tradition and esprit de corps, with rigorous training that instills deep senses of survival and honor. The presenter was a nonsworn civilian, and this particular situation occurred on the third day of a five-day training course. Rapport and trust were strong, participants were engaged, group dynamics were very positive; the class was going really well.

Evidence of such positive group dynamics was revealed by the participants' focus on the work, their humor, their interactions with each other, and their openness to share learning experiences. The week, up to this point, was going tremendously well. Yes, up to this point. The content being discussed centered on the lesson design and the ways an instructor determines what to teach. The presenter was using Wiggins and McTighe's (1998) Understanding by Design model to illustrate the differences between enduring understandings, important to know, and nice to know.

In this specific situation, the group was focusing on developing the enduring understandings that are important to policing. An officer asked the presenter to give an example. The presenter responded by saying, "Law enforcement is unique in that one way of thinking about being an officer is that you have absolute authority to issue a death sentence without a judge. Given that idea, what might recruits say if asked the question, 'Why do police carry guns?'"

The group immediately shifted to stillness when the "Why do police carry guns" question was asked. The group of police officers, about 30 in the room, all stopped breathing. Their eyes became focused directly on the presenter, like a predator honing in on prey—rapport was instantly broken, trust had faded. The question was perceived as a socially liberal statement against law enforcement. The entire group shut down while at the same time their level of threat was heightened—this is not the psychological state a presenter wants the group to be in, especially in a room full of armed individuals!

Clearly in this class, the meaning of the presenter's communication was not what the presenter intended; rather, it was the response received. The shift in group dynamics, rapport, and trust was so dramatic that it seemed there was almost no way out. As I watched the presenter begin to flame out, I remembered a line I once read in *Presenting Magically* (James & Shephard, 2001): "There are no resistant audiences, only inflexible presenters" (p. 37). The urgency to become more flexible was imminent.

In this case, the presenter's flexibility was demonstrated by a direct and open admission to the officers. The presenter explained the original intention behind asking the question: to surface the enduring understanding connecting democracy and the U.S. Constitution to the role of law enforcement and the need to have firearms to protect those who cannot protect themselves and to ensure for all citizens the freedom granted by the Constitution. This was coupled with an honest and sincere statement expressing deep respect for the officers and the work they do. When the presenter acknowledged that something was amiss and then reframed the context, rapport and trust were back on track. It has been two years since that event, and some of the officers recently e-mailed the presenter to reflect on that moment and how they have successfully used the skills learned from that class in their own academy courses.

The reason for sharing this story now and not in the chapter on recovering with grace is to surface the importance in recognizing when a response does not satisfy the group. It offers a not-so-subtle example of responding inappropriately. Whether the reaction is extreme or subtle, the participants' microexpressions are the same. Recognizing and processing the incoming data informs the presenter of the response given and is vitally important in determining what to do next. As effective presenters, we all know that data is neither good nor bad; it is simply data. Sometimes we may mistakenly apply judgment to data or we may get emotionally caught up in the group's response. These reactions are not useful because they can decrease our flexibility. We use data to inform, not to judge the quality and effectiveness of our presentations, responses, credibility, and all the qualities essential to a great presentation.

So what does responding appropriately look and sound like when initially done well? What is a presenter doing when responding appropriately? Earlier in this book, we mentioned that the 7 Essential Abilities are presented as discrete abilities to support your leaning. We also mentioned that these abilities are richly dynamic within the complex world of human communication and relationships. This is especially true in the case of responding appropriately, which is an ability that is closely associated with acknowledging and responding as well as recovering with grace. For instance, as a presenter, your response is influenced by how you acknowledge, and in some cases your response may be a recovery, like the story about the police training. In that example, the response-and-reframe was a recovery move.

## THE VERBAL COMPONENTS OF RESPONDING APPROPRIATELY

Responding appropriately has two components: the content of the response and the nonverbal choreography. Let's explore the content first. The content of your responses is guided by the participant's question or comment. When a participant asks a question, you respond with the content that best answers the question. Garmston (2005) offers a useful frame when listening for questions. Consider four possible question types: true-false, multiple choice, short answer, and essay. As you listen to the question and mentally assign it a question type, your response will be structured in a way that best addresses that type.

For a true-false question, responding by saying "Yes" or "No" followed by a brief explanation is generally acceptable. For a multiple-choice question, you first restate the correct option and then offer a brief explanation of why it is the best answer. The response to a short-answer question is a short answer, from one word to one sentence. The response to an essay question is a brief statement of fact followed by an elaboration (for examples of responses, see Garmston, 2005, p. 106).

As a subject matter expert, your expertise and experience may be why you are presenting in the first place. Participants, wanting to learn, will ask you questions in the hopes that the content of your responses will be useful. By recognizing the question types, you can save time, stay focused, and satisfy the intellectual curiosity of participants—all while maintaining credibility and rapport.

The second component of responding appropriately, the nonverbal choreography, is important because how you say your response can make the difference between a well-received one and a poorly received one. The following story deals with the impact of how something is said on a group's dynamic.

### GROUP 1, PRESENTER 0 = A LOSS OF CREDIBILITY AND RAPPORT

Human communication is complex, dynamic, and unpredictable. As presenters, we have our models of human behavior, our presentation skills, and a lifetime of experiences. Yet even with all these assets, we can find ourselves in trouble. This story reveals a situation in which a presenter's beliefs overshadowed and contradicted the data generated by the group. The outcome was a shift to lower perceptions of credibility coupled with decreased group member participation.

At a regional university in California, we were participants in a two-day session on communication led by two nationally recognized presenters with very respectable credentials and reputations. The audience included university faculty, administrators, and staff whose experience at the university ranged from 1 to over 20 years.

In the morning of day one, group energy was high and attention was directed toward the presenters. The group responded within seconds when the presenters asked them to "turn to your neighbor and discuss. . . ." The small-group conversations were steady, lively, and on topic. The shift from presenters presenting to group members processing ran smoothly throughout the morning. But after lunch, an interesting shift developed that rapidly led to a discombobulated session. As we sat and watched, we realized this was a moment of rich learning revealing what not to do.

The content shifted from theory and content to role-playing so that participants could practice the skills. Specifically, the shift was from assertive questioning techniques to scenarios in which they applied the skills in real-life situations. As the exercises continued, questions emerged from participants. One question in particular caused a significant shift resulting in decreased rapport between presenters and participants as well as a decrease in the group's perception of the presenters' credibility. The shift was significant enough that the group turned against the presenters.

The presenters were experts in their content and had written numerous books and articles. They had been, up to this point in the session, excellent presenters. They had established and maintained rapport and credibility, and developed positive group dynamics. Everything had seemed to be going well. The group had responded well to questions, provided powerful follow-up comments, gone into and come out of activities quickly, and stayed on task throughout the morning. Then it happened: a participant asked a question.

When presentations shift to freefall, questions from participants are often the catalyst. Questions are interesting linguistic constructs that greatly influence our state of mind. When a question is asked, no matter the intention, it can be perceived as a threat. In an intellectual sense, questions live very close to the emotions related to challenge and the reactionary response to defend. Many of us have had experiences in which someone asked us a question that we perceived as a challenge. The perceived challenge may be to our subject matter expertise, our credentials, our content, or any number of other factors. The perceived challenge can be cognitive or emotional. An example of a cognitive threat is when a participant asks a question that overtly challenges the content and may require the presenter to defend a particular stance. An example of an emotional threat is when a participant asks a well-intended question and the presenter perceives it as a challenge. If the presenter shifts to an emotional state, he may become trapped in an associated state, unable to separate himself from the emotional barbs of the question. When that happens, the presenter downshifts. His breathing becomes more rapid and higher in the chest, and his voice volume and speech pace may increase. The tone of his voice shifts off baseline and elevates. When the elevated tone is accompanied by high breathing, the message is often perceived as anger or pleading, and this is exactly what happened in this session.

As you continue to read this story, you will discover the emotions that surfaced and the repression of participation. Keep in mind that we describe observable behaviors, and try not to assert the internal mental states of the presenters or the audience. This is important because when skillfully using the 7 Essential Abilities, your ability to observe and process data free from interpretation is of primary importance. Observing and processing the data without transgressing into why a person is doing something keeps you more flexible and proactive. When presenting, it is more effective and efficient not to ask why but rather to simply observe and process data, respond, observe and process the influence, and respond. By using an observe-process-react cycle, you remain present in the moment. If you were to focus on why a person responded a certain way, you might lose the moment and get bogged down in a conversation in which you try to convince a participant that she is not feeling how you think she is feeling. It is a vicious cycle when that happens—as you shall now discover.

A participant raised her hand and, with a rhythmic voice tone, palm-up gestures, and fingers slightly curved, said, "You know, I disagree. I don't think this will work. Were I to do this to a bully, they would probably go to the boss and have my head." Midway through this statement, one of the presenters, maintaining direct eye contact, began moving toward the participant. The presenter stopped about six feet from the participant, the closest either presenter got to a participant who made comments or asked questions in a whole-group arrangement. This comment was different from the comments during the morning segment, which had all been of the clarifying and probing types whereby participants were seeking clarity about the content. The presenters' responses in the morning were contextually rich and received with open minds.

As the participant finished her sentence, the presenter raised a hand up from the side to a level equal to her waist. The forefinger was extended so that she was pointing at the participant, and with a credible and succinct pace, she said, "No" and continued with "You need to think about how to make this work for you. . . ."

The participant continued, "Yes, I understand, but I don't see this working here. Our problems are unique."

The presenter responded emphatically, "This will work here. You need to try it and experience the success. If you can't, then rehearse it with a colleague you trust so you can do it right when it counts."

As the two were engaged in their verbal tennis match, the group was being entertained by the participant's lobs and the presenter's slams. Like a cat whose tense and piercing focus fixates on potential prey, the group was transfixed on the interaction, watching with tense stillness, waiting for the kill shot.

The group was revealing lots of useful data, which was passing through the air and past the presenters with no detection of concern on their radar. Like the tree that falls in the woods for no one to hear, the group data was passing by the presenters as if they were not there. Why? Because the presenter engaged in this back and forth was too close to the participant to see the group; she had lost her peripheral line of sight and was thus blind to the group. This is the equivalent of a blind spot on radar. Radar works well above certain elevations, but when an object drops below a certain altitude it becomes invisible to the system. When presenters come too close to the "target" they lose connection with the group. In this case, the presenter was responding to the participant without regard to the group's reactions and perceptions. She was flying blind—she was looking at a tree and could not see the forest.

Other than watching the exchange between presenter and participant, you might be asking yourself, "What was the audience doing?" Watching the group from our perch, we noticed several things. First, the group froze when the presenter first responded with "No." They stopped moving and breathing, and they directed their visual attention to the presenter. We know from Chapter 2 that once people stop breathing, they decrease their cognitive faculties and downshift. The presenter did not see this because she was too close to the participant and she, too, had downshifted.

After a few seconds, the group moved slightly; heads turned toward others at their tables. Participants did not completely turn to their partner, but just slightly turned their heads while continuing to look at the presenter. Grinder (2008) calls this group response "shocked," and it is important to be able to see this pattern, recognize it, and know how to respond to it. There was little evidence that afternoon of the presenters seeing it, recognizing it, and responding to it.

Within 90 seconds, the exchange was over and the presenters moved on to the next part of the session. What was interesting for us to see was the shift in behavior. For the rest of the afternoon, the group was not as compliant and focused as they had been in the morning. When the presenters asked participants to "turn to a neighbor" or "begin the activity," the group took three times longer to get on task than they had that morning. More people were off topic than before, as evidenced by the collective group voice volume. When the presenters called the group back at the end of an activity, participants did not immediately comply and the compliance was not in unison as it had been in the morning. And perhaps most surprising was that after this brief conflict, participant comments and questions stopped completely. When the presenters asked the group if anyone had questions or comments, no one asked a question or made a comment. After the deafening silence, the presenters would say, "Good, let's move on."

This is a vivid example of how to respond *in*appropriately. We have seen it many times, and yes, we have done it ourselves—the responsible party leaping head first into the abyss of presenter's hell. Chapter 7 provides some concrete skills to extract ourselves from the abyss; however, this chapter is about responding—and in this case, responding inappropriately.

In this chapter we have presented two stories. One illustrated an appropriate response pattern, and the other illustrated an inappropriate, or less effective, response pattern. In both cases. the participant's and presenter's intentions were most likely positive, but they are not relevant because intention does not change the data. In the second story, we believe the intention of the participant was to increase her understanding and learn how to apply the skills. The intention of the presenter surely must have been to support the participant's thinking and encourage her thinking. Yet the data says otherwise.

On a continuum of group data, we can plot breathing, movement, and eye contact. The continuum for breathing is from low to high, for movement it is from still and rigid to smooth and flowing, and for eye contact it is from indirect to direct. As breathing becomes shallower, eye contact more direct, and movement decreases, the group's level of receptivity and emotional safety decreases.

## RESPONSE EXPECTED = RESPONSE GENERATED

From our perspective, we know our response is appropriate when the response we get is the response we expect. You may have expected us to say that we know our response is appropriate when the response we get from a group includes low breathing, fluid movements, and engaging eye contact. We said it the way we did because there are times in training sessions when your intention may be to shock or annoy because you are modeling a strategy or technique. Or perhaps it is to connect with the group. For instance, we saw one presenter, who was presenting to a group of high school teachers about student achievement scores from the statewide assessment and what to do about them. The presenter opened the session with this statement: "Today we are going to look at test results that you will not like. I don't like them either. In fact, I thought this was bull!" The group froze, stopped breathing, and stared at the presenter with the same stare a deer gives when it stops in the middle of the road and is staring down a set of headlights. In this case, the presenter had the group right where she wanted them—initially shocked by revealing a common belief that she shared with the group, a belief that the test data was "bull." The shock was in hearing it come from the presenter, an expert in assessment and data analysis. The next statement was brilliant, and it shifted the group from where they were to a level of high receptivity with lower breathing and fluid movements: "There was good reason I thought this was bull. I did not understand the connection between the data and my teaching. What might you think about these results if a relevant and useful connection linked your teaching to student learning in a formative and useful way? By understanding those links, you can make a difference in student performance." By the end of this monologue, the group had shifted back to the state that the presenter wanted. She responded appropriately by getting the desired responses.

The choreography accompanying the opening statement was eloquent. The presenter initially established a presentation location. She paused, took a step, and named the resistance in a strong credible voice. She paused and took half a step back toward the initial location. Then, using an approachable voice, she reframed the message in a way that appealed to a common value teachers have—the belief that effective teaching affects student achievement. She then returned to the initial location, and the group was fluid, calm in their breathing, and had direct eye contact with her. A quality session was well on its way.

What this presenter did was respond to the group's nonverbal display of resistance. The group was resistant most likely because the teachers did not respect the state assessment and were disappointed in the student achievement results. The presenter addressed the resistance by naming it and then reframing it in a way that opened the group's level of permission to consider the data and how it might help them improve student learning.

## Practice 6.1 | Increasing Peripheral Vision

*Most recommended:* This exercise is best done with a partner. You are the presenter, and your partner is a participant. Have the participant raise his hand. As you scan the room, walk to the side of the front stage opposite the participant's location and then call on him. What do you notice about your view of the rest of the room, especially if it is full of participants?

*Less recommended:* Using the same setup, this time when the person raises his hand, walk toward him and then call on him. What do you notice about your view of the rest of the room, especially if it is full of participants?

## SUMMARY

✓ To preserve a group dynamic that supports a safe learning environment, attending to the audience is the most important responsibility.

✓ Responding appropriately has two components: the content of the response and the nonverbal choreography.

✓ When presenters come too close physically to the "target" (i.e., participant making a comment or asking a question), they lose connection with the group and cannot read the group effectively.

✓ Maintaining your consciousness in the observe-process-react cycle, you are more resourceful and do not get bogged down in the why.

✓ As participant breathing becomes shallower, eye contact more direct, and movement decreases, the group's level of receptivity and emotional safety decreases.

# 7 Recover With Grace

*Perfection comes not from excellence in the delivery, rather from grace in the recovery.*

The effective presenter knows the elusive nature of flawlessness and accepts that perfection is not in the science of delivery but rather in the art of recovery. The effective presenter is not flawless; the effective presenter is flexible and strategically recovers with deliberate grace. We begin this chapter with anticipated excitement as we explore our favorite ability. Why is this our favorite? Because recovering with grace is the one ability that keeps you present in the moment. It sits patiently within your consciousness—ready at a moment's notice to dance across the stage when disaster is imminent. This ability is about how to be vigilant by always monitoring, adjusting, and responding not to your own intentions, but to the group's reactions, because the meaning of your communication is not in the intent, rather it is in the participants' meaning. As professional developers, we must be aware that there also is no perfect lesson when training. The importance of our intentions is that they drive our attention, which drives our behaviors. Because we believe this to be true, having conscious awareness of how to recover, how to make the group "right" is one of our primary responsibilities.

Oscar Wilde once said, "The play was a great success, but the audience was a disaster." As a presenter, your sessions, no matter how well designed and well executed, are deemed effective only by the judgment of the participants. Just as there are no resistant audiences, only inflexible presenters, there are no disastrous audiences, only inflexible presenters.

Flexibility is the energy source that mobilizes your ability to make choices when your anticipated reaction does not align with the participants' actual reaction. So you adjust, you recover. It is our view that this essential ability is ever present because you are constantly adjusting as you strive for an elusive state of perfection. Perfection is not a destination; is it the journey. The skills that support recovering with grace are changing location, interrupting yourself, decontaminating, amnesia, and break-and-breathe. These skills are grounded in the assumption that you can create a state of amnesia in the audience such that they are not conscious that an error occurred. That state is impacted through the use of two important elements, location and pattern shifts, which carry two important assumptions. One is that location has memory, and the other is that by changing patterns you can create a psychological distance between what you want to do and what you did.

## LOCATION HAS MEMORY

Let's first explore the idea that location has memory. We know from research in the fields of education and psychology that memories are strongly linked to emotions. As we recall the most significant events in our lives, the memories of those events not only have content, they also have stored with them the emotional state we were in when we had those experiences.

One excellent example is for you to think back to a special evening when you were dancing with the one you love. Contained in your memory of that evening are the song, the building you were in, the aura of romance, the lighting, and perhaps even a memory of sweet perfume. You may even be able to remember the whole dance as if you were watching your own mental movie of it. You can remember the closeness and how you moved as one. As you think of that occasion right now, you might feel the love from that moment today even if it took place decades ago. Emotions anchor our memories and ensure that they stay with us for a lifetime.

Another delightful example many of us have experienced is our wedding day. This time, as you recall your wedding day, think more specifically about a single moment, something specific about the day. It may be the moment you were pronounced husband and wife, a dance during the reception, or perhaps a conversation with someone special in your life. Take a minute and think about a moment from that special day. Once you have selected the memory, think about what you are remembering. Is the memory in vivid color? Do you hear a special song or a warming voice? Is it a memory recalled as a movie or a series of photographs? Now recall the emotion of the memory. As you do, notice how more alive and vivid the memory becomes. Often, you may remember what you were wearing, the details of the room, or the surroundings if you were outside. You may even recall the time of day and the weather. On rare occasions, if you can remember a scent also, it becomes the most vivid of all memories.

Now try to do the same thing while thinking about what you did three or four days ago. Preferably, think of a day when nothing particularly eventful happened. Chances are, your memory does not have the vivid details like your wedding day, and therefore little is remembered.

Depending on your generation, there are also tragic events that occurred, and we know exactly what we were doing, what we were wearing, and who we were talking to when they happened. I am old enough to remember such a day that happened in November 1963. I remember where I was sitting, what was on TV, the weather, and what my mother was cooking when President Kennedy was shot. If you are younger, it may be the Challenger explosion in 1986. Of course, as Americans, we all have memories of September 11, 2001. Location has memory.

Still not convinced? Consider this: have you ever walked into a room and forgotten why you did so? And what do you do next? You turn around and go back to where you came from. Why? Because the memory is in the room where you started, and you return to that location to retrieve the idea.

By knowing that location has memory, you can use this to your advantage when presenting. You read in an earlier chapter how to use location to anchor memory and accelerate learning. Here you will learn how to use location, especially a change in location, to create amnesia, recover, and anchor new memories.

Let's consider a simple example that has most likely happened to all of us while presenting: starting a sentence we wished we hadn't. When that happened to you, what did you do? Prior to knowing these skills, I used to stop midsentence and say, "Never mind, that is not what I meant to say" or "Ah, let me rephrase that." In some cases, I even went on to complete the ridiculous statement because I did not know what else to do. No matter which option emerges, there is nothing inherently wrong with any of them. But none of these creates a state of amnesia and disappears in the minds of the participants.

When starting a sentence you wished you hadn't, and you are in a situation in which credibility and rapport must be maintained, there is a way to recover such that the audience does not know you made an error and are recovering. On the surface, the move is simple: stop talking, take a silent step or two, and start the sentence you want to say. At a deeper level, there are several micropatterns to incorporate with tempered nuance in order to really pull off a smooth recovery with group amnesia. The text box nearby lists the skills in sequence.

**Creating Amnesia**

1. Stop talking.
2. Breathe and close your mouth.
3. Use a frozen hand gesture.
4. Break and Breathe: As you take a step, exhale, break eye contact with the audience, and drop your gesture.
5. Silently take a step or two.
6. Step into the new location, and pop up with a different gesture and voice tone as you make eye contact with the group.
7. Start a new sentence.

The first step is to stop talking. And to create the image that you are still being thoughtful and steeped in brilliance, when you do stop talking you must also breathe and close your mouth. This may sound easy, but we have found that more often than not, when people stop talking in the middle of a sentence they often stop breathing with their mouth open as if in the middle of a word. Silently standing still while not breathing with your mouth hung open is not considered to be a particularly intelligent look. If you don't believe us, take a break for a moment. Find a mirror and look into it. As you look at yourself, say, "That is not what I meant." At the end of the sentence, stop breathing and leave your mouth open for about three seconds. How does that look to you?

So back to our presentation. You've stopped talking, and you are breathing low while extending a frozen hand gesture in front of you. After a second or two, as you begin to exhale, simultaneously break eye contact, drop your gesture to your side, and silently take a few steps. Once you sense that you have walked far enough, literally step into the new location and rapidly pop up with a gesture different from the one used in the old location. This move is what Grinder (2008) calls Break and Breathe (see Figure 7.1). The well-executed Break and Breathe is very important to creating amnesia because, when done well, this move separates the old pattern from the new pattern that is about to emerge. For instance, if you gestured with your right hand in the old location, use your left hand in the new location. Every pattern you change in the new location increases the intensity of participants' amnesia. How many steps you take depends on how much amnesia you want to create. There have been times when one of us walked halfway across the stage, remaining silent while walking for five or six seconds.

You may be wondering how you can know whether this pattern works. To understand how it looks, let's return to the old location where you started a sentence that you did not want to finish, so you stopped and held your breath. If you could have seen the group when this happened, you would have noticed that they, too, stopped breathing when you stopped breathing. The group mirrors the presenter. One thing we know from previous chapters is that a group that is not breathing is a group that is not receptive to ideas. A group that is not breathing is a group whose

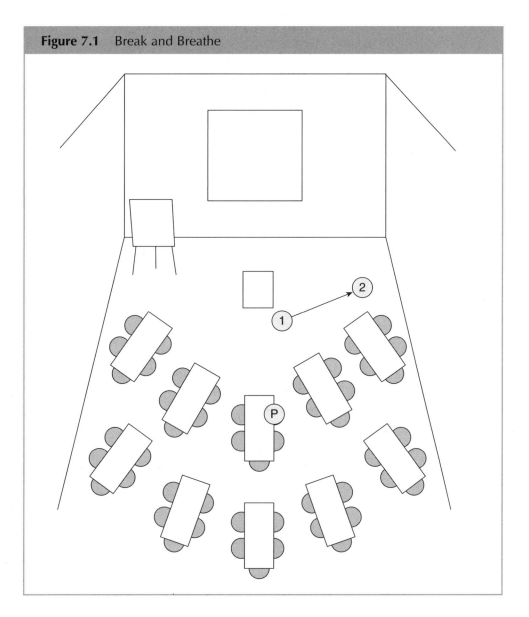

**Figure 7.1**  Break and Breathe

mental state is not where it needs to be in order to support thinking. Seeing your audience in that state means it is time to recover.

We begin with the Break and Breathe because it is at this point in the recovery dance that you get the group to breathe. When a recovery move works, the group continues to breathe and may even mirror your breathing and head nods. Because of this, when you reach the new location, the group is okay. As you start your new sentence, you notice that participants are attentive and breathing low, and that there is fluidity to the waves of movement across the room—they are in sync with you. When this happens, recovery is graceful and effective.

## WHEN THE RESPONSE GIVEN IS NOT THE FAVORED RESPONSE RECEIVED

Another moment for recovery is when you respond to participants' questions or comments. This phase in an adult learning environment is precarious because not only do you have to satisfy the person who asked the question or made the comment, you must also satisfy the group. Respectfully responding to a participant's comment or question is important for maintaining credibility and rapport. And no matter how carefully constructed your response, you run the risk of having your response fall short of the participant's expectations. You want to satisfy the participant's intellect and maintain the relationship, so it is important to first recognize when he is not satisfied.

Sometimes participants tell you by saying, "No, that is not what I asked," or they may briefly stop breathing or moving. As you notice the nonverbal shifts from fluid to rigid or from breathing to not breathing, it is time to recover with grace. The same Break and Breathe pattern used earlier is also effective in this situation. As participants shift to stillness, it is time to break rapport and recover. So, pause, break, and then breathe. Take a step or two, and pop up with nonverbal patterns different from the original location and a new response. Now that a new location has been created, you can do the following choreography to really separate yourself from the old location, the poor response, and the reduced credibility.

When you first step into the new location, point to the original location and, using a credible voice, say, "That response missed the target." Then pause and gesture to the new location where you are standing and say, "Here is another perspective . . ." and continue with your new response. You will know how effective the Break and Breathe is by watching the participant who asked the question and seeing whether he has refocused and is continuing to fully listen to you.

## WHEN THE GROUP REACTS

We believe that one of the primary responsibilities of the presenter is the emotional safety of the group. Groups respond, nonverbally, to participant questions and comments. We have all been in an audience when someone asked an inappropriate question, talked too much, or simply took a path that no one was interested in. When that happens, groups react. Grinder (2008) suggests using a technique called Satisfy-Satisfy-Delay when specifically responding to three group behaviors: shocked, confused, and annoyed.

A group that is shocked by a participant comment or question is a group that collectively stops breathing for a moment and tends to freeze or at least move with less fluidity (see Figure 7.2). When a group of participants displays this behavior, they are not sure what is going to happen next; they are shocked and thus not emotionally safe. As presenters we want to make the group "right" by bringing them back into a state of receptivity. Our goal is to get them to breathe, and the most effective way to do that is to respond to the comment or question in a positive manner (see Figure 7.3). If it was a comment, consider paraphrasing for clarity and to surface the participant's thinking about the

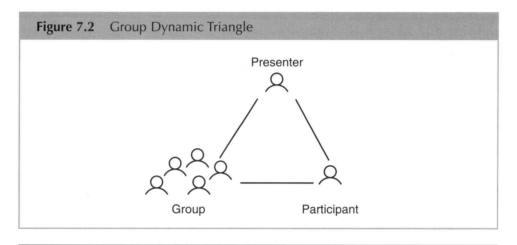

**Figure 7.2**   Group Dynamic Triangle

*Source:* Grinder, 1997.

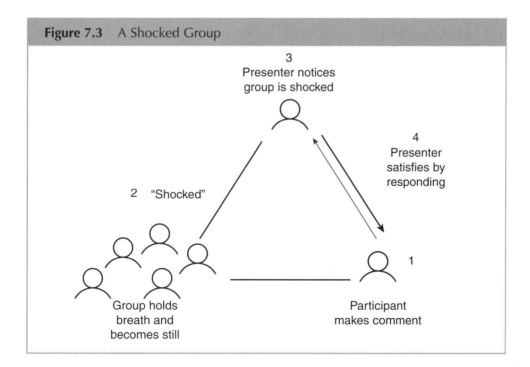

**Figure 7.3**   A Shocked Group

connection between the comment and the session content. If it was a question, simply answer it briefly and succinctly.

Groups that are confused have a similar emotional state to groups that are shocked—they do not feel emotionally safe and do not know what is coming next. Groups displaying a state of confusion are very subtle in their behavior. Confused group members slowly begin to turn their heads toward the person seated next to them, often while keeping their eyes on the presenter or the person making the comment. They never fully turn to their neighbors; they simply begin to turn, often while holding their breath. So the best indicator of a confused group is partial turning in addition to holding their breath (see Figure 7.4). In this situation, the most effective thing a presenter can do is get the group to refocus and breathe. This is best done using the same pattern used for a shocked group: satisfy them by responding in earnest. When the presenter does this effectively, participants will return their focus up front, they will breathe, and a rhythmic fluidity will return to the group.

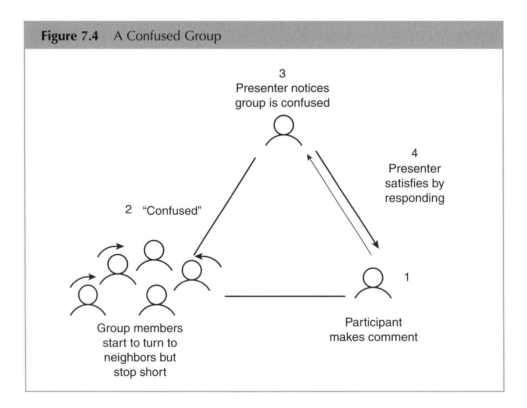

**Figure 7.4** A Confused Group

3
Presenter notices
group is confused

4
Presenter
satisfies by
responding

2 "Confused"

1

Group members
start to turn to
neighbors but
stop short

Participant
makes comment

Eventually some groups can get annoyed with a participant (see Figure 7.5). You know the one who shows up periodically in the session you are attending—the one who incessantly asks questions, makes comments, or challenges the intellectual credibility of the presenter. The annoyed group is the group that finally goes auditory. A group that is annoyed often makes "tsk tsk" noises. Participants in this group may fully turn to their neighbor and make a sound, side-talk, roll their eyes, or shake their heads. The annoyed group wants the presenter to take control and shut the disrupter down so the session can continue, as it should. The way to deal with an annoyed group is for the presenter to delay the response. The delay might be the statement, "Hold that idea, and you and I can talk during the next break." When the presenter does this well, the group will often shift in their seats, refocus their attention on the presenter, breathe deeply, and increase their attention, as evidenced by sitting up straighter in their seats. At this point, they are satisfied with the delay because they know the presenter knows they want to get back on track. The person who asked the question is satisfied because she often looks forward to talking with the presenter during the break. And yes, you do need to talk to the person during the break.

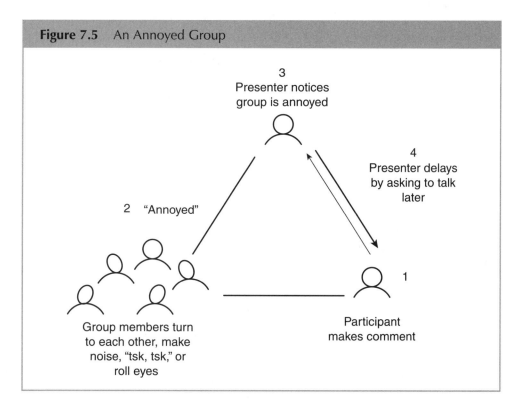

**Figure 7.5**  An Annoyed Group

3
Presenter notices
group is annoyed

4
Presenter delays
by asking to talk
later

2    "Annoyed"

1

Group members turn
to each other, make
noise, "tsk, tsk," or
roll eyes

Participant
makes comment

One final important point to make about Grinder's Satisfy-Satisfy-Delay pattern has to do with the voice pattern, gesture, and pause used when delivering the delay statement. The presenter should make this statement in a credible voice while standing still and breathing calmly. Adding a palm-down gesture is another factor that often ceases additional comment from the participant. Finally, after the statement is delivered, a brief and eloquent pause at the end is a deafening crescendo of power that further takes the wind out of the sails of the participant to ensure no additional comments will be made soon.

## THEY ARE NO LONGER LISTENING

"Pay attention!" In adult learning environments, that comment would most likely not go over too well with the group. Our thinking is that direct management of adult groups is, as a rule, inappropriate. So how do we recover when the group stops listening? From one perspective, it doesn't really matter why they stopped listening. What is important is to quickly and smoothly get their attention back in a way that maintains high levels of receptivity and cognitive engagement.

What does it look like when a group is no longer listening? Well, it can look like a hundred deer staring into the headlights. And it's not always that obvious. A subtle pattern can be a shift from fluidity of movement to more rigid or stiff movement. It might be the group shifting in their chairs or an interruption caused by a phone ringing, a person getting up, or a wave of yawning rushing across the group. There are infinite causes behind why a group stops listening. But when they do stop listening, it is time to recover with grace and make the group right by bringing them back into a state of receptivity.

One way to get the group's attention is by inserting a shift in the pattern of delivery that is large enough to impact the unconscious mind and small enough to not trigger the conscious mind. One of our favorite moves is I Interrupt Myself, a variation to the ABOVE (pause) *whisper* pattern introduced in Chapter 4.

When you find yourself in a situation in which participant attention has waned, then interrupt yourself early in a sentence, maybe two or three words in. You might even use a louder voice volume for those two or three words before pausing. The shifts from loud to silent and from fluid to stiff represent two significant shifts in patterns. Since we know the brain has a high acuity for recognizing pattern shifts, once the pattern shift is recognized the unconscious mind kicks in and increases attention. The increased attention is often seen in behaviors such as direct eye contact, dilation of the pupils, erect posture, and a shift to increased stillness. Once you have participants' attention, you can return to your baseline patterns.

| Practice 7.1 | I Interrupt Myself |

Stand in one location while gesturing with your right hand, and say in any voice tone, "Using this strategy. . . ." Then pause for three seconds, and take one step to the side. Pop up your left hand to gesture, and using a different voice tone and pace, say, "Using this strategy to get the group's attention is effective because of the radical shift in pattern." The following exercise is an advanced technique that is so effective it can actually draw a person out of deep daydreaming. This is an actual midword interruption using the same script as above with a slight variation.

| What to Say | What to Do Nonverbally |
|---|---|
| "Using this stra-" | As you say the line, use a regular or slightly quicker pace than your baseline pace, and gesture with your right hand. |
| | Stand still, breathe, and hold the gesture still. |
| | Exhale and take a step while simultaneously breaking eye contact and dropping the gesture. |
| "Using this strategy to get the group's attention is effective because of the radical shift in pattern." | Pop up with a left-hand gesture, and in a whisper say the first three words. Slightly pause between each word, and move your hand in a downward beat motion during each of the three words while freezing the gesture during the brief pauses. Then continue the sentence, with your voice slowly increasing in volume until you reach your baseline pattern. |

## DECONTAMINATING WHEN IT IS NOT YOU

Because memory has location, there are times when the memory is so awful that the location has to be decontaminated, at least nonverbally. One such situation that we have experienced several times has nothing to do with the presentation. Instead, it has to do with history. Working with school districts, it is not uncommon to present in the boardroom. In some districts the boardroom has the ghosts of memories past. For instance, it may be the room where a vote to strike was taken. And that is precisely what happened in one school district where I (Kendall) was asked to present. I knew that the strike vote was traumatic and that residual negative emotions were still lingering when my session was scheduled.

I arrived early and specifically asked to have a portable screen available. I had the room set up in the opposite way than it had been when the strike vote was cast. So the old front of the room was now the back of the room. I never went to the back of the room and kept the focus in the new front location. By changing the orientation of the room, I decontaminated the hostile location and the group was receptive and positive.

Perhaps you are wondering if it was even necessary to go to all the trouble of rearranging the room? Well, some years back I did not do my homework and walked into a situation in which the training room also happened to be the room where the school board had made the decision to close two elementary schools due to budget cuts. The result was that students had to be bused and several teachers and staff lost their jobs.

The day of the training, the room was set up the same way it had been for that fateful board meeting. As teachers walked in, there was a detectable aura of low energy. I started the training, and the energy remained low—everything I tried seemed to fall short of picking up the energy in the room. It was a challenging morning, and by lunchtime I was exhausted. At lunch I found out what had happened in that room two months prior to this training. What a fantastic moment! I rushed back to the room and rearranged it so the new front location was not in the same orientation as the old front location where the tragic news of school closures was delivered.

As people walked in after lunch, they scanned the room and found new seats. I was standing at the side of the room in a location where I had not stood during the morning session. After getting their attention, I began by saying, "It was in this room [pause; gestured to the old front of the room] that news about significant changes in your district was delivered. [pause] The most difficult news: school closures. Jobs are lost, children are relocated to new locations, some separated from old friends [pause; walked to the new front location where the presentation was now being delivered, and said in a passionate pattern] and that is why today is so important. The work we do today will make a difference to the children because it will help create a more welcoming and nurturing environment for them." The rest of the day was energetic and full of participation, with people smiling for the first time that day. Does location have memory, and can it influence a group? Absolutely. And when it does, recovery is necessary and decontamination is the most effective move.

## WHEN YOU REALLY STEP IN IT

The previous example was initiated by an event over which the presenter had no control. What about a situation in which you actually may have been the cause of the ill feeling? For us, self-deprecating humor is often effective while decontaminating. One situation that comes to mind is when the group is being somewhat playful with the presenter. This may result in you making a statement to which someone in the audience calls out and responds, "That's not true" or "You've got to be kidding." To recover, break and breathe, take a step, and then in a somewhat exasperated voice, while pointing to the old location, say, "Ha, I would never say that!" Then, pointing to where you are standing, say, "What I would say is . . ." and then continue with your response. Laugh a bit. Groups respond well to the playful back and forth.

## WHEN YOU LOSE YOUR PLACE

Who among us has not lost their place during a presentation? Or perhaps come to the realization in the moment that a particular PowerPoint slide would be very helpful in explaining a concept. Better yet, the computer freezes up! One common experience we have witnessed many times is when the presenter goes auditory with her internal dialogue. It may sound like, "Let me see. Hold on one minute while I find that slide. No, that isn't it. I know it is here someplace. Hmmm. No. Oh, I know where it is. . . ." This can seem to go on for an eternity. As the presenter searches frantically, she may look up at the group and realize in a moment of stunned fear— "Oh my, they are staring at me!"

What to do? Our suggestion is, of course, to recover! An effective way to recover is to not go verbal with your internal dialogue. Rather, consider saying, "Turn to your neighbor and for the next 52 seconds share what you think is the most important point from the past hour." Or go into an activity that is brief and requires little setup. We often have several easel papers pre-prepared with quick activities such as Matchbook Definitions. The exit directions are simple: "If you could summarize your learning thus far with a statement that would fit on a matchbook, what would you write? Create a Matchbook Definition and be prepared to share it with the group. You have five minutes." Or you could give participants four minutes to talk with their table group members and create a list of questions they have thus far. When the four minutes are up, ask them to come to consensus on two from the list. The reason we ask them for two is so that the group has a backup in case their first question was already asked.

Then while the group creates their products and no one pays attention to you, you can calmly locate the item you were looking for while not involving the group in your anxiety. Recovery becomes invisible, and the group is none the wiser.

I (Claudette) once presented to a group of administrators and superintendents who had just completed a self-assessment in which they had rated their own behavior vis-à-vis their application of agreed-upon group norms. After they shared this inventory with a partner, I addressed the whole group: "What might need to happen for you to increase your use of selected norms when working with that group?" As soon as I finished the question, I knew I would get no responses because the group had collectively stopped breathing. I quickly came to the realization that I had created a situation with far too much risk. I had asked them to share their self-assessment with all of their peers and their supervisors, and they were letting me know that it was not safe enough for them to risk. I broke eye contact, walked to a new location, and popped up and started again: "Please turn to your partner and share what might need to happen for you to increase. . . ." They started talking to each other right away. In the initial design of that segment, I had not considered that the participants might require the psychological safety that is provided by working in pairs. Thankfully, recovery is much more important than perfection.

| Practice 7.2 | Recovery With Grace |
| --- | --- |

Think of a situation in which you "stepped in it." Briefly describe the situation in the space below:




Using some of the strategies from this chapter, choreograph a recovery specifically addressing your personal situation.

## SUMMARY

✓ Location has memory, and by changing patterns you can create a psychological distance between what you want to do and what you did.
✓ The well-executed Break and Breathe is very important to creating amnesia because when well done, this move separates the old pattern from the new pattern that is about to emerge.

✓ Groups can exhibit three stages of behavior in response to a participant comment: shocked, confused, and annoyed. The Satisfy-Satisfy-Delay strategy can be useful in each of these stages.

✓ One way to get the group's attention is by inserting a shift in the pattern of delivery that is large enough to impact the unconscious mind and small enough to not trigger the conscious mind. One of our favorite moves is the I Interrupt Myself, a variation to the ABOVE (pause) *whisper* pattern introduced in Chapter 4.

# Notes

1. McCafferty (2002) asserts the role of gesture in and of itself and in conjunction with speech in creating zones of proximal development (Vygotsky, 1978) for second language learning and teaching.

2. Milgram, Dunn, and Price (1993) posit that one of the most important aspects of instruction is the student-teacher relationship. Forming this relationship is dependent on the ability to develop rapport.

3. The following researchers have published papers about the influence of nonverbal communication patterns on thinking, memory, and insights into reading what people are thinking: Alibali, Flevares, and Goldin-Meadow (1997); Bower (2005); Brekelmans, Wubbles, and Creton (1990); Church and Goldin-Meadow (1986); Cooley and Triemer (2002); Gaythwaite (2005); Goldin-Meadow (1997, 2003, 2004, 2006); Goldin-Meadow, Kim, and Singer (1999); Goldin-Meadow and Mylander (1998); Kendon (1997); McNeill (2000); Phelps, Doherty-Sneddon, and Warnock (2006); Roth (2001); Scherr (2003); Zoller (2008).

4. The concept of barometers was first introduced by Michael Grinder (1997) in *The Science of Non-Verbal Communication*. He posits that specific individuals in a group are the first to react to humor, content, boredom, break time, and other stimuli that influence attention. By recognizing the barometer (i.e., the first person to react), the presenter can interrupt the wave of interference and maintain a positive group dynamic with higher levels of participant attention.

# References

Alibali, M. W., Flevares, L. M., & Goldin-Meadow, S. (1997). Assessing knowledge conveyed in gestures: Do teachers have the upper hand? *Journal of Educational Psychology, 89,* 183–193.

Bennis, W., & Biederman, P. W. (1998). *Organizing genius: The secrets of creative collaboration.* Reading, MA: Addison-Wesley.

Bloom, B. (1956). *Taxonomy of educational objectives: The classification of educational goals.* New York: Longmans, Green.

Bower, B. (2005). Hands-on math insights. *Science News, 167*(3), 36–37.

Brekelmans, M., Wubbles, T., & Creton, H. (1990). A study of student perceptions of physics teacher behavior. *Journal of Research in Science Teaching, 27,* 335–350. doi:10.1002/tea.3660270405

Caine, R. N., & Caine, G. (1994). *Making connections: Teaching and the human brain.* Boston: Pearson Learning.

Church, R. B., & Goldin-Meadow, S. (1986). The mismatch between gesture and speech as an index of transitional knowledge. *Cognition, 23,* 43–71. doi:10.1016/0010–0277(86)90053–3

Cooley, E. L., & Triemer, D. M. (2002). Classroom behavior and the ability to decode nonverbal cues in boys with severe emotional disturbance. *Journal of Social Psychology, 142,* 741–751.

Costa, A. L., & Garmston, R. J. (2002). *Cognitive coaching: A foundation for renaissance schools.* Norwood, MA: Christopher-Gordon.

Csíkszentmihályi, M. (2003). *Good business: Leadership, flow, and the making of meaning.* New York: Penguin Books.

Doyle, M., & Straus, D. (1976). *How to make meetings work* (Jove ed.). New York: Berkley.

Dunn, R., & Griggs, S. A. (1988). *Learning styles: Quiet revolution in American secondary schools.* Reston, VA: National Association of Secondary School Principals.

Ekman, P., & Friesen, W. (1969). The repertoire of nonverbal behavior: Categories, origins, usage and coding. *Semiotica, 1,* 49–98.

Gardner, H. (1985). *Frames of mind: The theory of multiple intelligences.* New York: Basic Books.

Garmston, R. (2005). *The presenter's fieldbook: A practical guide.* Norwood, MA: Christopher-Gordon.

Garmston, B., & Wellman, B. (2009). *The adaptive schools sourcebook* (Vol. 1, 2nd ed.). Norwood, MA: Christopher-Gordon.

Gaythwaite, E. S. (2005). Didn't you see what I meant? *Curriculum and Teaching Dialogue, 7*(1/2), 97–108.

Ginot, E. (2009). The empathic power of enactments: The link between neuropsychological processes and an expanded definition of empathy. *Psychoanalytic Psychology, 26,* 290–309.

Glickman, C. (1998). *Human will, school charters, and choice: A new centralized policy for public education.* Unpublished manuscript, University of Georgia, Athens.

Goldin-Meadow, S. (1997). When gestures and words speak differently. *Current Directions in Psychological Science, 6,* 138–143. doi:10.1111/1467–8721.ep10772905

Goldin-Meadow, S. (2003). *Hearing gestures: How our hands help us think.* Cambridge, MA: Harvard University Press.

Goldin-Meadow, S. (2004). Gesture's role in the learning process. *Theory Into Practice, 43,* 314–328. doi:10.1207/s15430421tip4304_10

Goldin-Meadow, S. (2005). The two faces of gesture: Language and thought. *Gesture, 5,* 241–257. doi:10.1075/gest.5.1.16gol

Goldin-Meadow, S., Kim, S., & Singer, M. (1999). What the teacher's hands tell the student's mind about math. *Journal of Educational Psychology, 91,* 720–730.

Goldin-Meadow, S., & Mylander, C. (1998). Spontaneous sign systems created by deaf children in two cultures. *Nature, 391,* 279–281. doi:10.1038/34646

Goleman, D. (2006). *Social intelligence.* New York: Bantam Books.

Grinder, M. (1993). *ENVoY: Your personal guide to classroom management* (2nd ed.). Battle Ground, WA: Michael Grinder and Associates.

Grinder, M. (1997). *The science of non-verbal communication.* Battle Ground, WA: Michael Grinder and Associates.

Grinder, M. (2008). *The elusive obvious.* Battle Ground, WA: Michael Grinder and Associates.

Grinder, J., & Bandler, R. (1975). *The structure of magic.* Palo Alto, CA: Science and Behavior Books.

Gumm, W. B., Walker, M. K., & Day, H. D. (1982). Lateral eye movements to verbal spatial questions as a function of questioner location. *Journal of General Psychology, 107,* 41–46.

James, T., & Shephard, D. (2001). *Presenting magically: Transforming your stage presence with NLP.* Bancyfelin, Wales: Crown House.

Kendon, A. (1997). Gesture. *American Review of Anthropology, 26,* 109–128.

Kendon, A. (2004). *Gesture: Visible action as utterance.* Cambridge, England: Cambridge.

Luft, J., & Ingham, H. (1955). The Johari window: A graphic model of interpersonal awareness. In *Proceedings of the Western Training Laboratory in Group Development.* Los Angeles: University of California, Los Angeles.

Mast, M. S. (2007). On the importance of nonverbal communication in the physician-patient interaction. *Patient Education and Counseling, 67,* 315–318. doi:10.1016/j.pec.2007.03.005

McCafferty, S. G. (2002). Gesture and creating zones of proximal development for second language learning. *Modern Language Journal, 86,* 192–203. doi:10.1111/1540–4781.00144

McCafferty, S. G. (2004). Space for cognition: Gesture and second language learning. *International Journal of Applied Linguistics, 14,* 148–167. doi:10.1111/j.1473–4192.2004.0057m.x

McNeill, D. (Ed.). (2000). *Language and gesture*. Cambridge, England: Cambridge University Press.

Milgram, R. M., Dunn, R., & Price, G. E. (Eds.). (1993). *Teaching and counseling gifted and talented adolescents: An international learning style perspective*. Westport, CT: Praeger.

Phelps, F., Doherty-Sneddon, G., & Warnock, H. (2006). Helping children think: Gaze aversion and teaching. *British Journal of Developmental Psychology, 24*, 577–588. doi:10.1348/026151005X49872

Piaget, J. (1963). *The origins of intelligence in children*. New York: W. W. Norton.

Poyatos, F. (2002a). *Nonverbal communication across disciplines: Volume 1: Culture, sensory interaction, speech, conversation*. Philadelphia: John Benjamins.

Poyatos, F. (2002b). *Nonverbal communication across disciplines: Volume 2: Paralanguage, kinesics, silence, personal and environmental interaction*. Philadelphia: John Benjamins.

Poyatos, F. (2002c). *Nonverbal communication across disciplines: Volume 3: Narrative literature, theater, cinema, translation*. Philadelphia: John Benjamins.

Rizzolatti, G., & Gallese, V. (2002). fMRI study of actions (deliverable D2). *Information Society Technologies, 1*, 16.

Rosenthal, R., Hall, J., DiMatteo, M. R., Rogers, P., & Archer, D. (1979). *Sensitivity to nonverbal communication: The PONS test*. Baltimore: Johns Hopkins University Press.

Roth, W.-M. (2001). Gestures: Their role in teaching and learning. *Review of Educational Research, 71*, 365–392. doi:10.3102/00346543071003365

Scherr, R. E. (2003, August). *Gestures as evidence of student thinking about physics*. Paper presented at the American Institute of Physics Conference, Madison, WI.

Siegel, D. J. (2007). *The mindful brain: Reflection and attunement in the cultivation of well-being*. New York: W. W. Norton.

Silver, H., Strong, R., & Petini, M. (2008). *The strategic teacher: Selecting the right research-based strategy for every lesson*. New York: Prentice Hall.

Stamenov, M. I., & Gallese, V. (2002). *Mirror neurons and the evolution of brain and language*. Amsterdam, Netherlands: John Benjamins.

Vygotsky, L. (1978). *Mind and society*. Cambridge, MA: Harvard University Press.

Wells, G. (1999). *Dialogic inquiry: Toward a sociocultural practice and theory of education*. Cambridge, England: Cambridge University Press.

Westen, D., Blagov, P. S., Harenski, K., Kilts, C., & Hamann, S. (2006). Neural bases of motivated reasoning: An fMRI study of emotional constraints on partisan political judgment in the 2004 U.S. presidential election. *Journal of Cognitive Neuroscience, 18*, 1947–1958. doi:10.1162/jocn.2006.18.11.1947

Wiggins, G., & McTighe, J. (1998). *Understanding by design*. Alexandria, VA: Association for Supervision and Curriculum Development.

Willis, J. (2008). Building a bridge from neuroscience to the classroom. *Phi Delta Kappan, 89*, 424–427.

Zoller, K. (2008). Nonverbal patterns of teachers from 5 countries: Results from the TIMSS-R video study. *Dissertation Abstracts International: Section A. Humanities and Social Sciences, 68*(9-A), 154.

# Index

**CORWIN**

A SAGE Company

The Corwin logo—a raven striding across an open book—represents the union of courage and learning. Corwin is committed to improving education for all learners by publishing books and other professional development resources for those serving the field of PreK–12 education. By providing practical, hands-on materials, Corwin continues to carry out the promise of its motto: **"Helping Educators Do Their Work Better."**